To The Great Southern Sea

TO THE GREAT SOUTHERN SEA

Also by William Albert Robinson
10,000 Leagues over the Sea
   (published in England under the title *Deep Water and Shoal*)
Voyage to Galapagos

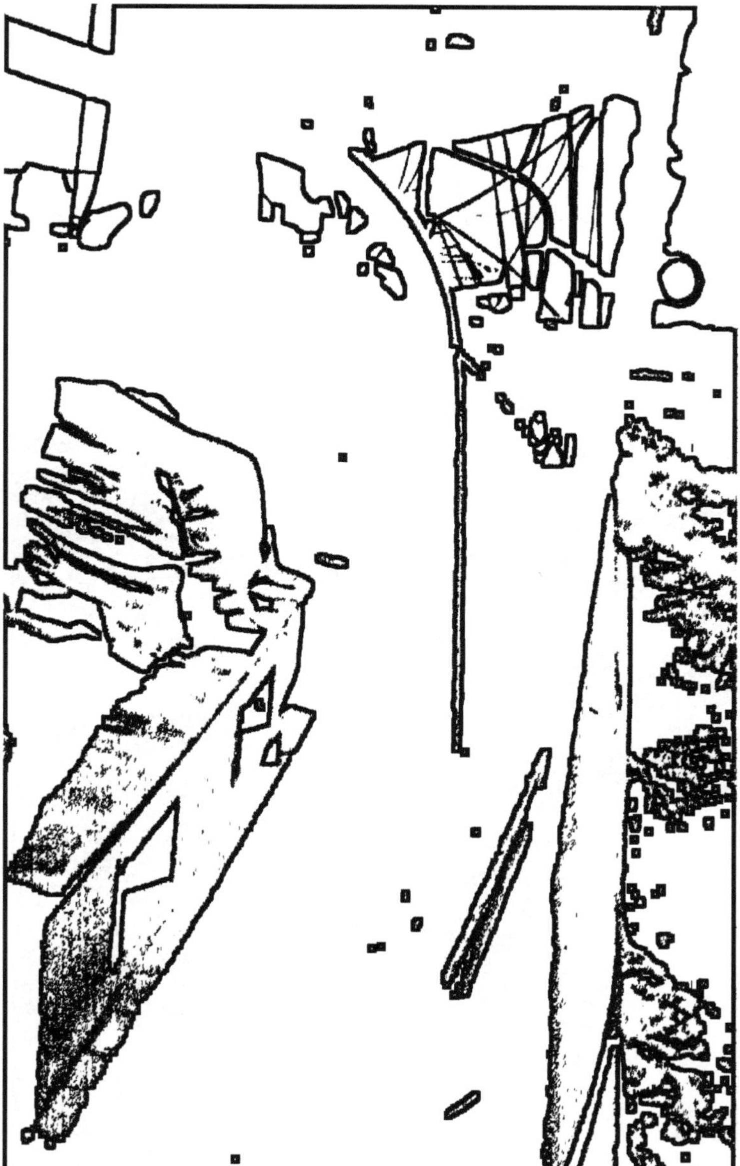

WILLIAM ALBERT ROBINSON

To the
Great Southern Sea

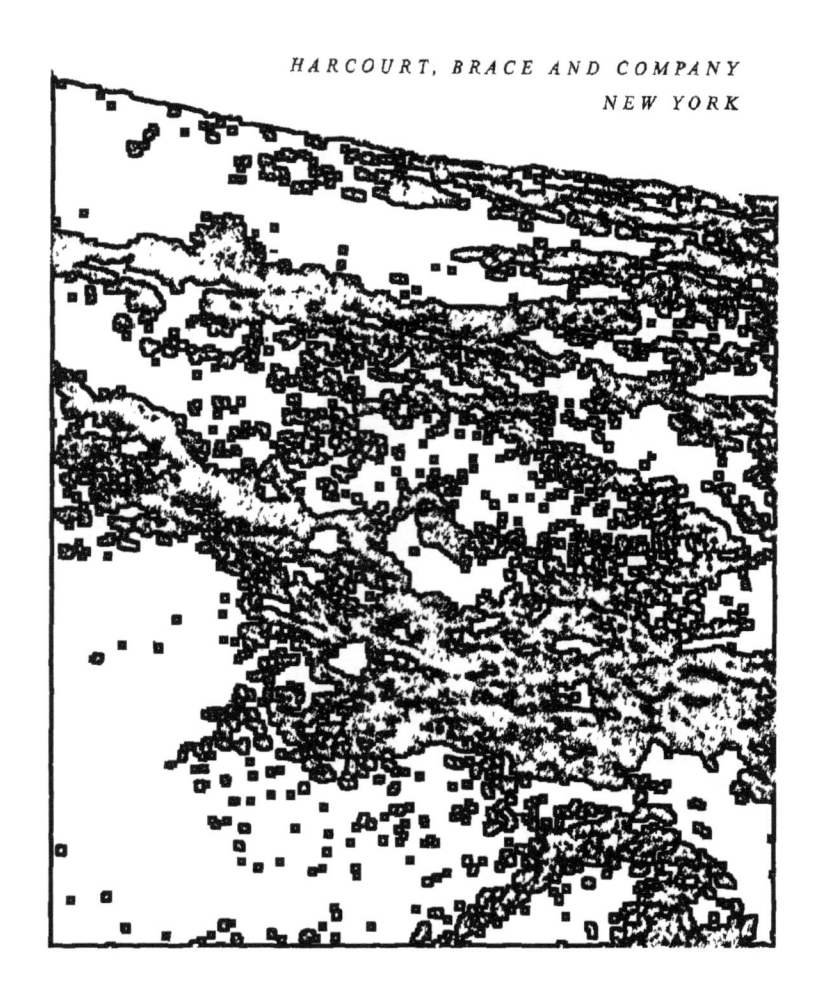

HARCOURT, BRACE AND COMPANY
NEW YORK

© 1956 BY WILLIAM ALBERT ROBINSON

All rights reserved, including the right to reproduce this book or portions thereof in any form

first edition

LIBRARY OF CONGRESS CATALOG CARD NUMBER. 56-6664

PRINTED IN THE UNITED STATES OF AMERICA

Parts of this book previously appeared in *Sports Illustrated* under the title "The Ultimate Storm."

THIS BOOK IS FOR HINA

Who was three months old, according to Ah You,
At the start of the voyage to the great southern sea

Who was born in Panama six months later
And went to sea in a basket at the foot of the mainmast

WHAT WENT BEFORE

It all began with a voyage around the world in the thirty-two-foot ketch *Svaap*.

I had gone directly out of engineering school into a good job in charge of research in a textile mill on the East River across from Manhattan. Prospects were bright—only, I was uneasily conscious that it was not my life.

Bound to give it a fair trial, I worked hard; but usually I spent the noon hour at the nearby docks where ships were unloading from Calcutta, Hong Kong, Kobe, and many other faraway ports. Evenings were spent poring over maps, or deep in the literature of early exploration. I began, in a small way, a collection of accounts of early voyages, which has been continued and expanded to this day. Week ends I sailed on Long Island Sound in a leaky old sloop I had bought, and practiced navigation out of books borrowed from the New York Public Library.

It took three years to be sure of what I wanted to do, and by that time I had saved the necessary money. Then I burned my bridges. The purchase of *Svaap* for $1,000 was a stroke of luck. She was a perfect little ship for what lay ahead. The distant horizons that beckoned were limitless, if somewhat vague. The main thing was that I was setting out to voyage, in my own ship.

The first voyage began in June of 1928. In the fall of 1931, *Svaap* tied up at the Battery in New York after having circumnavigated the world. It was during the voyage that

WHAT WENT BEFORE

I fell victim to what might be called "island disease," or in this case, more specifically, "Tahiti disease," for I knew that someday I would return and build my home there.

The book I wrote about the voyage was a success. There were magazine articles, apparently endless lecture engagements. I was astonished and gratified to learn that one could lead this kind of life and make a living at the same time. It seemed too good to be true. The future would be even more delightful, for I had married.

Svaap again sailed south, and through the Panama Canal; but this time she was loaded with motion-picture gear, for we were to make a film in the Galápagos with penguins and other small inhabitants of the group as actors. Afterward, we would sail to Tahiti. In the Galápagos, prepared to remain six months or more, we got off to a fine start. Our sets were built. Our small actors were lined up and had become accustomed to us . . . and I developed a ruptured appendix and was only saved by a miracle. The accident lost us *Svaap*, which had to be left in Galápagos and was confiscated and wrecked by Ecuadorians.

Forced to give up the film project, we went to Tahiti by steamer while I recovered my strength. Fate was smiling again and soon we were building our home—old Polynesian style, mostly terrace, cool under its wide pandanus roof— facing the lagoon at the mouth of a lovely little valley named Ofaipapa. A clear stream with innumerable waterfalls and fern-bordered pools came down from a hidden source deep in the heart of the mountains. There was plenty of room for a small plantation of coconuts, tropical fruits, and exotic flowers, and for the first time in my life I learned the joy of working on the land.

Almost anyone would have been content to stay and live peacefully ever after in a place so beautiful; but a strong

WHAT WENT BEFORE

New England conscience kept whispering that I must do something more serious with my life.

Thus, after two years I found myself back in New England with a small shipyard. My love for the sea and ships had been too strong to sever altogether, so I built ships instead of sailing them: schooners for the Gloucester fishing fleet; beautiful sailing yachts that took away with them, each time they left, a part of me.

When the sea urge got too strong again I took time out from the shipyard . . . and a few weeks later was bending sail in the little port of Kaits, between Ceylon and southern India, aboard a ninety-foot teakwood trading vessel named the *Annapooranyamal* for which I had paid 25,000 rupees —a little over $9,000.

For years I had remembered this beautiful little Ceylon-built brigantine I had seen while on the first voyage of *Svaap,* and after combing the coast from Colombo to Madras had found her in Kaits, just back from a voyage to Burma.

Inasmuch as one could hardly go sailing around the world in a ship with a name like that, I renamed her after my wife, Florence C. Robinson, and went exploring among the islands in the Indian Ocean, followed by the Red Sea and the Mediterranean. Back in Gloucester, Massachusetts, the five turbaned, white-robed Hindus who made up my most delightful crew, startled the ultraconservative townspeople by flying enormous musical kites from our anchorage in mid-harbor.

I would have made the final break then and sailed back to Tahiti in the *Florence C.,* but personal reasons made it impossible. So my wonderful crew went home to Kaits, and Valvettiturai, and the brigantine was sent to the Pacific,

WHAT WENT BEFORE

where she became a successful Papeete trading vessel. I continued with the shipyard.

Later, when conditions were at last propitious for leaving, Fate intervened again, this time in the form of war clouds. We began building mine sweepers, submarine chasers, and landing craft. After Pearl Harbor, almost before I knew what had happened, the little yard in Ipswich had twenty to thirty vessels building at a time, and six hundred men working twenty-four hours a day—and my old life in the Pacific was even more remote and unattainable than ever.

When the war was over, I was finally able to burn my bridges for good. I liquidated the shipyard. Sadly I said good-by to the loyal team of men and women who had turned out two hundred vessels in record time. Underneath the sadness of the parting was the knowledge that at last I was going back to the life that meant most to me, and that my ship lay waiting. For although the shipyard had taken years of my life it had also given me my dream ship.

She had been built just before the war and was nearing completion when it broke. Actually she was our schooling for the deadly serious work which was to follow, for in building her we had perfected a technique of composite steel and wood construction that was strong and light, and allowed maximum use of the space inside a hull. We built many ships for the navy by this same method.

During most of the war years I had lived aboard her in the shipyard basin to be close to the work. She had never been quite finished. We sailed for Tahiti still working on her. Not until she reached the Pacific, and lay at anchor off the island of Taboga in Panama Bay, did she have her complete and unique sail plan, designed and rigged to be ideal for trade wind passages, and capable of being handled by only two men. Its nearest counterpart is perhaps the Mediterranean polacca brigantine.

Her arrangement on deck and below included all the features I had planned carefully for years, developed specifically for comfortable living in the tropics. It included many things not usually found in a small ship, such as a real engine room and workshop, and a photographic laboratory. She was to have been about sixty feet over all but in order to get everything in had been stretched to seventy, with sixteen feet beam, and just under eight feet draft when fully loaded. She displaces fifty tons, and has a small heavy-duty diesel engine of forty-seven horsepower to get her through calms and in and out of ports and rivers.

Her performance under all conceivable conditions has exceeded even my optimistic expectations, and is a tribute to the ability of the two men who collaborated with me in her design: the late W. Starling Burgess, best known for having designed the *Ranger*—last, and probably greatest, of the America's Cup defenders; and L. Francis Herreshoff, dean of today's yacht designers.

Her name, *Varua*—Tahitian for spirit or soul, has a poetic ring when pronounced, and seems to express the essence of the ethereal beauty of a sailing ship, and her eternal quest. By the time we had reached Tahiti on her first voyage I knew that she was a dream ship come true. When at last she lay still and secure at the foot of Tahiti's green mountains, and we drove slowly out through Faaa, Punaauia, and Paea, and stood beside my long cool house looking out through the palms to Mooréa and the sunset, I knew that the rest of my dream had also come true.

People still come to Tahiti seeking something that existed two hundred years ago—the dream islands that Wallis, Cook, Bougainville, and all the others vied with each other in describing—incredibly beautiful islands that were a paradise on earth, peopled by a handsome golden-skinned race whose generous, loving nature became legendary.

Fifty years ago Gauguin painted Tahiti, and became famous a generation later, about the same time that several books were written about the island in a sort of alcoholic reverie. The picture that exists in the minds of many is formed by this source material.

Tahiti in mid-twentieth century is not the Tahiti of the time of Cook, or even of Gauguin. Beneath the truly staggering beauty of the islands there are tragic undertones such as filariasis and elephantiasis; on my return I became almost immediately involved in a medical research campaign against them, and now, after several years, it is possible to hope that they will soon disappear, leaving a heavy incidence of tuberculosis as the sole remaining great medical objective.

Tahiti is not a logical place in which to live. Life here requires a high degree of self-reliance. It is difficult and expensive to get to Tahiti and the cost of living is high. Niceties and everyday luxuries and conveniences that are usually taken for granted are missing. Routine matters such as getting your plumbing fixed involve astonishing complications. True, Tahitian girls are still as broadminded as they were in the days of Cook, but that is not a very solid foundation on which to build a life here.

But Tahiti is not the dissolute, degenerate place painted recently by certain individuals who make a living by writing sensational exposés, and who seem to get all their material from the Papeete bars and two or three disillusioned habitués.

This is still a land inhabited by a gentle, happy Polynesian race, protected from exploitation by a paternal

French colonial policy. All of the original beauty of these fantastic islands, which was here when Cook and the others passed, is still here, as is the cloud of low islands out there in the sea over the horizon—infinitely small fragments of beauty thrust up from precipitous ocean depths.

There is something about island life. You can only get there by coming over the sea or through the air, which makes your piece of earth very special. The Japanese have a theory about what they call "island psychology" which applies just as well here, for it is quite true that one's whole attitude toward life changes when one lives on an island.

Then there is the climate, overlooked in the usual hysteria about love and romance: a climate close to perfection, unless one misses winter.

It was here that I had put my roots down years ago—my first real roots; here that I labored, built, and planted. Coming back in 1945 those roots went still deeper.

When I first cleared my valley it was an eerie feeling to uncover ancient tikis, long abandoned *fei* plantings, dead orange trees, far up near the headwaters of the stream. In the years since then, I have put much of myself into the valley, which is becoming a tropical botanical garden of exotic fruits and flowering plants and trees. Besides the many things for ourselves, including innumerable varieties of hybrid hibiscus which we have introduced, there are tropical cherry trees planted expressly for the almost extinct wild pigeons, who are coming back; and there are seed trees for the smaller birds. The doves we brought from Honolulu on one voyage are established now too, and their soft call wakes us in the morning. Recently we have added the Barro Colorado jungle trees, the Panama tamanu, and other booty from the Chile voyage.

Today my valley is lush and fruitful. I wonder how long

it will be after I am gone before it is again impenetrable bush, like the valleys of the ancient Tahitians, like mine when I first found it in 1934.

Of late I have added to the comforts of Ofaipapa. There is a sound-proofed diesel generator. With electricity we even have hot water now, and good music; and can sit by the ironwoods in the evening with Tchaikovsky floating out from under the thatch roof, while the flaring torches of the fishermen move across the lagoon on silent canoes.

There was everything I had ever dreamed of, only—as it had been years ago when it all started—I began to wake up at night and go and study the charts. And when I went aboard *Varua* I knew that she was too splendid a ship to be making tame voyages around Oceania and to Honolulu.

A plan began to take shape. For years I had hoped someday to cross the southern ocean on the old sailing ship track, where the big square-riggers used to run their easting down to the Horn, and where the great winds blow unceasingly and the seas roll on around the world unhampered. None of my previous ships would have allowed me to think in those terms—for I had no desire to make the voyage as a stunt in an unsuitable ship—but with *Varua* I had the ship.

For years also, I had wanted to follow the Humboldt Current from its source off southern Chile until it lost itself three thousand miles later in the Pacific beyond Galápagos.

The passage across the southern ocean and the voyage along the Humboldt could be combined. During 1951 plans crystallized.

Toward the end of the year we would sail south from Tahiti as far as was necessary to reach the great passage-making westerlies. There we would run down our easting—and having had that great experience, and no real reason for wanting to go on around the Horn, would break the voyage in southern Chile. If it was early enough in the season we would explore Patagonia briefly, but only as a side issue, for that might be a complete project for another day.

From southern Chile we would join the Humboldt, which would take us the whole length of South America, along the colorful desert coast of northern Chile and Peru and through the fantastic bird islands, to Panama, and then to Galápagos. Afterward there would be the peaceful trade wind passage back home to Tahiti.

And so the decision was made; all that was lacking was the date. In Papeete Harbor, sheltered by Fareute Point and Motu Uta, lay *Varua,* waiting.

CONTENTS

What Went Before ix
1. South of the Sun 3
2. Rapa 15
3. The Great Southern Sea 26
4. The Ultimate Storm 57
5. Landfall 75
6. Valdivia and the South 92
7. River in the Sea 108
8. Panama and the New Apprentice 141
9. Southbound Again—Tumaco 151
10. Galápagos 161
11. Mangareva and Home 172

APPENDICES FOR THE PRACTICAL SAILOR
 I *Varua:* conception, design, construction, equipment, etc. 199
 II The Storm 223
 III Riding Out a Storm 225

ILLUSTRATIONS

PLATES (*following page* 136)
    Varua off Tahiti
    Ah You
    Zizi and Piho with dorado
    The author in *Varua*'s saloon
    Tino
    Varua's sails etched against a graying sky
    Varua drives south against unexpected head winds
    Close hauled, *Varua* leaves Panama
    Varua sails upriver to Valdivia with pilot aboard
    Varua at rest, Valdivia
    Varua in smooth waters
    Fishermen of Huanchaco with *caballitos*
    Fishermen's miniature church, Lobos de Afuera
    Enrique shows his birds to Ah You and Piho
    Hina in her basket at the foot of the mainmast
    Hina and Ah You at the penguin village, Elizabeth Bay,
        Galápagos
    Tino and the belligerent sea lion, Galápagos
    Tomb of Maputeoa, last King of Mangareva
    Everything furled and under power for the calm of the last
        three hundred miles
    Approaching Tahiti at the end of the voyage

DIAGRAMS
    Varua's sail plan   214
    Varua's deck plan   216
    Varua's ventilation   218
    Varua's accommodation plan   220

TO THE GREAT SOUTHERN SEA

1. SOUTH OF THE SUN

We sailed from Papeete on the last day of the old year, 1951, bound for the great southern sea and Patagonia, after exhausting every conceivable excuse to linger in Tahiti. Last trips up the valley had become a joke. My affairs were in order as much as they ever would be. To have had the best weather for the coast of Chile we should have left in October. I have no idea how it got to be December, and *Varua* still on her mooring in Papeete.

Finally in desperation, with the new year only a few hours away, I loaded the camionette to the roof with our personal gear, gathered my little band together, and we tore ourselves away from Paea where our cool shaded house stood looking out across the blue lagoon to the west and Mooréa, and the little stream—swollen from the recent rains—rushed noisily down the lush green valley through its pools and falls.

It was actually a spurious departure, with things temporarily stowed and chronometers not even running—but at least we said good-by to the two or three friends who knew we were leaving and got away from insidious Papeete without farewell scenes. Then, instead of putting out to sea, we went around to a favorite anchorage on the other side of the island where we were pretty sure no one would find us—where we had another excuse to bathe a last last time in a Tahiti river before sailing for the less seductive world.

But more important than enjoying an extra day or so of

the beloved island, there was the serious business of making the ship ready for her greatest test. *Varua* was in splendid shape, already checked and rechecked; but even so I wanted one more chance, with no Papeete distractions, to go over every detail of rigging where failure might occur, for I had just had a shocking object lesson of what can happen. The magnificent 136-foot schooner yacht *Vega*, on which over a hundred thousand dollars had just been spent supposedly putting her in tiptop shape, had sailed from Tahiti only a little while before for Honolulu, to limp back to Papeete a few hours later, totally dismasted because someone had neglected to check two of the most important fittings in the rig. Where we were going one did not come back from such accidents—there are no ports of refuge in the Roaring Forties.

So out there, anchored off the mouth of a wide clear river behind a delightful little *motu*—just a speck of an islet big enough for a few dozen coconut palms—I went over the ship minutely, examining every foot of gear and rigging and every fitting from the end of our long bowsprit to the tips of our stern davits—and on up to the very top of the masts. We made a good deep-water stow of all our gear and supplies, started the chronometers on Greenwich time by radio time tick. When all the work was done we just sat and looked at Tahiti—watching the late afternoon clouds form around the dark green mountain where a long feathery waterfall dropped from a notch high up to form the river in which we swam at sunset. For a last time we breathed the cool perfume of the land breeze coming out to us with the night.

Tino, who had just signed the Blue Cross Pledge for the duration of the voyage and could therefore be trusted implicitly not to take a drink and fail to return, rowed ashore to leave two or three last letters with a nearby Tahitian family for mailing. One of them was a forgotten dentist's bill for a full set of false teeth which had been a present for Poona, a girl I hardly knew but who was a dream of an *ori* dancer. She had needed them to dance as the star of our district in the recent fete. Civic duties in Tahiti sometimes take on odd aspects.

Tino and the Blue Cross, false teeth for Poona . . . I went on to think of the things that bind one to Tahiti. Besides basic things like my valley and stream I found myself thinking of all the ridiculous things that could happen only in Tahiti and nowhere else. I thought of the wonderful fat women sitting in rivers weaving wreaths, their enormous bosoms floating melon-like in front of them in the current. I thought of the grandmothers roaring down the road with flying gray pigtails on powerful American motorcycles; of the little *Mitiaro* coming in from Mooréa practically sinking under her load of pigs and cows and bicycles and humans; of the plane that came to inaugurate the airmail service and got all the way back to the Cook Islands after the ceremonies before someone discovered she had forgotten to take the mail. I thought of the fishing dogs, and the high-flying hens who live in our mango tree; and of Hiria, our dappled gray horse, who likes to go to the beach to roll in the sand and swim in the lagoon on Saturday afternoons. We were never sure whether she kept track of the days or could tell it was Saturday by the cars on the road, nor could we understand why it had to be Saturday afternoon and not Sunday—unless she was a Seventh-Day Adventist horse and celebrated Sunday on Saturday. In any case she made an unholy fuss if forgotten, and eventually would jump the stone wall and go on her own, something she would never dream of doing on weekdays.

Sometimes I think all who live in Tahiti—animals, birds, and people—are a little crazy, and myself a little more so; for it is hard to explain why anyone in his right mind would want to leave Tahiti and the world's most wonderful climate to sail five thousand miles through the Roaring Forties over the most deserted and unpleasant stretch of ocean in the world—to visit Patagonia and the world's worst climate.

The two days spent on the other side of the island from Papeete gave the new crew a chance to get adapted to the ship and to each other. The complex details of life ashore were replaced by a single preoccupation—the ship and the forces of nature that affected her. Although it was New Year's Day when we tackled the job of making the ship ready for sea, and ashore the whole island was celebrating, all fell to with a will for they were as anxious as I to get under way. As we worked I could almost feel the little group welding together into what was to be a smoothly functioning team. From the moment we left Papeete until the end of the voyage ten months later, I never had a single doubt or regret concerning my crew.

We were five souls aboard. Tino was in his forties, big, darker than most Polynesians, unquenchably good-natured. Like most of the best sailors in Tahiti he came from the island of Rapa, southernmost of the islands of French Oceania. It was his first voyage on *Varua* although he had been to sea all his life on local schooners.

Zizi was a Tahitian and about the same age as Tino. He had already made one voyage to Honolulu and back on *Varua*. He was cook and sailor in about equal proportions, more at home in a galley at sea than in a house ashore. He was at times moody and could then be heard venting most effective hissing epithets at his stove or the soup; but like Tino he was always cheerfully ready to be called on deck day or night to handle sail or take his watch at the wheel.

We were on that intimate basis that exists between employer and employee in Tahiti, where people only work for you if they enjoy it and not for the money. Tino and Zizi lived up forward of the watertight bulkhead that separated the galley from the forecastle, in compact but comfortable quarters with their own facilities and complete privacy—which makes such a great difference in the contentment of crews aboard ship.

Aft, sharing our one spacious stateroom with me, was *Varua*'s new mistress, Ah You, who had never before quitted the solid security of Tahiti to venture farther than the barrier reef in quest of *maoa*. Her features and character, including probably her courage, were inherited from her maternal grandmother, who as a girl in the royal court of Siam had dared to run away with a visiting Cantonese to venture far from her known world—the temples and canals of Bangkok. Where they went is uncertain, but the grandchildren found themselves seven thousand miles east of Siam on the lush island of Tahiti. There the ninth child of a too-numerous brood was given to adoptive Tahitian parents who took her as a month-old baby to live in the remote district of Faaone on the windward side of the island. As is often done in Tahiti, she was given a French name, Philomène, in addition to her birth name Ah You. Although everyone else calls her Philo, I always use Ah You because I think its Oriental quality suits her better.

In the quiet valley of Faaone that cuts far into the mountains behind the village, Ah You had wandered most of her twenty-one years like Rima, following the secret trails where the ancient Tahitians once lived but where only the wild pig hunters went today. Often she would follow the river, flowing musically over its mossy stones, to the waterfall and the cliff where the fairy terns came to nest. Along the way she would climb for exotic forgotten fruits planted long ago. Coming back she would swim in the deep clear pools and rest on the grassy banks weaving wreaths of sweet-smelling *maiere* ferns while her long shining black hair dried in the sun.

Often she would go on the lagoon with her Tahitian father and thus learned the ways of the fish and all the other edible inhabitants that lived in the coral gardens and on the reef. She knew the names of every species and the name of the special nights of the moon when they could be caught, just as she knew the lore of the great valley. Of the outer world she knew very little, except the strange imaginative mind-pictures she had formed since she came to live at Ofaipapa in Paea. But all one hundred and ten pounds of her were quiet determination to see the world and not to be afraid of the sea.

Lastly, there was irrepressible eleven-year-old Piho, who at the age of seven had been given to us as a present by her people in Raroia, a remote atoll in the Paumotus. Children in the islands are probably more loved and spoiled than anywhere on earth, but also are constantly being given back and forth, becoming *faamu*. Teen-age girls will promise each other their first-born as a sign of devotion. Parents with children will feel sorry for childless neighbors or lonely couples whose offspring have grown up and gone away. A house without children is sad indeed—so what is more selfish than to hoard what your neighbor lacks.

Faamu children graft so quickly and naturally onto the new family stock that within a short time one would never dream they were adopted—all of which is probably a shock to non-Polynesian fathers and mothers, confident in their children's dependency on them and love for them exclusively. There is no such thing in these children's minds as their *real* family. All are real. It is just that they have more than the single one usually allotted to children elsewhere; and far from lacking security, it is doubled.

Thus it was perfectly natural for Piho's parents in Raroia —seeing our childless state, and noting how the child had attached herself to us during our stay—to give her to us as a parting gift, when we sailed for the Hawaiian Islands, to keep as long as we wished or for always. It was just as natural when we reached Honolulu and found that I was going to be away for many months on my filariasis work, to loan Piho to a warmhearted Hawaiian family. The children had become her friends, and the parents immediately became her Mama and Papa Paoa.

So now Piho is apt to talk about the time when her Mama told her this or that or did this or that, and while it is perfectly clear in *her* mind which Mama she means you don't know whether it is Mama Raroia or Mama Paoa. And now there was Mama Philo, as she called Ah You.

The same confusion attends the conversation of Ah You at times, for although possessed of only two fathers and mothers she talks about them as if they were one—which is, of course, distressing to my precise American mind that wants to know *which* one.

Piho lived here and there on *Varua,* depending pretty much on the weather. She loved to roll up in her blanket in the lee of the charthouse where she would sleep through almost anything including squalls, spray, and being walked on. Other times she slept in the transom berth at the foot of the chartroom companionway. In really bad weather she was ordered to a snug retreat off the galley. She was never seasick on the entire voyage.

Zizi was exasperating in the matter of cleaning his galley but able to cook in the worst possible weather, somehow able to leave his cooking without accidents on a moment's notice to haul on halyards or downhauls in a squall. Tino was tireless, able to smother an unruly topsail alone up on the mast, full of solicitude when Ah You was seasick, often letting me sleep through my dawn watch when he knew I was tired. Ah You, prostrate the moment the weather was bad, ate her meals determinedly only to lose them ten minutes later, but propped herself up hopefully with the guitar the moment the sea went down. Piho was ready to do any job any time for anybody, her boisterous laughter cheering the ship in low moments. Ah You, Piho, Tino, and Zizi were as dissimilar as the four winds. I sailed full of confidence in both crew and ship, and there was never a cross word or complaint even in the stress of the far southern days when continuing gales drove us nearer and nearer the ice drifting up from Antarctica.

The plan was to sail south, or as near south as the trade permitted, until reaching the Roaring Forties where we would run four thousand miles before the prevailing westerlies to the Patagonian coast. It was to be my first experience with the Great South Sea of the early navigators, which is not to be confused with the tropical "South Seas" of today's literature.

The only break in the five thousand miles to Chile was Rapa, nearly seven hundred miles south of Tahiti. Of ill repute due to its gusty anchorage, Rapa would not be a very relaxing interlude, but at least it would break the voyage. We could get a few fresh things there, and top off our water tanks. Tino would have a chance to revisit his native land for the first time since he left it as a youth to go to sea.

With a light breeze from the east we made sail as we left the pass in the reef. I gave the wheel to Ah You to keep her from feeling the wrench of leaving home too hard, but in a few minutes she wanted to go below. Later, just as the sun was setting, a curtain of rain moving in from the east began to blot out the already hazy green mountains behind us—but she was still down below. The rest of us were gazing astern, silent, wondering how long it would be before we saw our island again.

"Better come and see Tahiti once more before it's gone," we called down to her.

There was a moment of silence and when she answered her voice was unsure.

"I don't want to see Tahiti. I can't bear it." And she stayed below. Her courage was a little shaky just then. When the wind in the squall reached us and the sea began to rise, she was sick. It was the cross she was to bear from then on for the better part of six weeks, with only a few days' respite.

Soon it was night. The old beacons were there overhead, nostalgic of other voyages. The Southern Cross was ahead of us this time—good to steer by. Orion was setting in the west; a bright planet rising to windward. Astern was the wavering phosphorescent line of the long, long trail we would spin out day after day through calm and storm—the only, slight, momentary impression that the passage of *Varua* would make on the immensity of the sea.

The miles slid by, with the trade wind on its best behavior even though this was the unsettled season. The days were long, for it was midsummer in the southern hemisphere.

Dawn came at 4 A.M. Irregular hours and night watches became the natural way of life. As of old, my day began with the dawn watch, 3 A.M. to 6 A.M., and when the weather was reasonable it was the favorite part of my day.

I picked up the threads of navigation after a lapse of two years, with an English nautical almanac—the only one I could get—instead of the old familiar American one. The tables were differently arranged; the equation of time was reversed. I did some very careful cross-checking to be sure I had it right—then resumed my old time-saving tricks: taking sights on the even hour so as to use the tables without interpolation; calculating the time of meridian passage to the minute while working the morning sight, to save time at noon. Every few minutes saved from navigation or ship work meant that much more time to catch up on sleep or to relax with a book.

We sailed easily and steadily south; but whenever the controlling restraint of the easterly trade weakened, the southerly swell was there, breathing slowly and deeply. Even this far north there was ominous power in that long persistent swell.

At noon the third day out the sun was directly overhead—so close to 90° that it was impossible to tell whether to point the sextant north or south—and I wrote zero in my workbook for the zenith distance and used the declination as my latitude. Thenceforth we were south of the sun; south of the Tropic of Capricorn as well, for the first time in my life.

It was a most unnatural state of affairs, this heading south into the great empty southern sea with nothing but the isolated pinpoint of Rapa between us and the Antarctic. The growing moon was astern; the constellations all in the wrong places. Piho, who had spent her whole life in one latitude, except for the voyage north to Hawaii, came to me all mixed up.

"The sun should not be there—but here," she said, pointing up.

I agreed rather too heartily—it being already noticeably colder—wondering just how good an idea the whole thing was anyway.

The most unnatural part of all was that things were behaving too well. On the exact dotted line where the pilot chart indicated "Southern Limit of Southeast Trades" the trade died, after having behaved like an angel. For a few hours the sea smoothed out except for the long swell from the south. Poor Ah You, who had been unceasingly seasick, appeared on deck and sat at the wheel with her guitar, hoping fervently Rapa had a river to bathe in and wash her hair.

"Aué—mes cheveux!" she wailed. All her life she had lovingly washed and tended that long black hair every day. To do it properly took gallons of water and I had explained that once a week would have to do until we were near the coast of Chile. I think that burden was the worst she had to bear during the voyage—worse even than the seasickness, which was at least in part due to her condition, and her condition was that which would bring joy to any Tahitian girl.

Both Tino and Zizi, wanting to please like all good Polynesians, assured her that in Rapa we would all bathe in a river.

We had less than two hundred miles to go now. A few very heavy and long-drawn-out squalls developed from nowhere, bringing us slowly nearer Rapa, through more than a hundred miles of very heavy cross seas which Zizi claimed were always encountered in that area. Zizi had made the voyage to Rapa as cook on the government schooner *Ta-*

mara several times, and was thus the authority on this region instead of Tino, who had been born down there but had left it for good twenty-eight years ago.

Piho, delighted to be given free rein in her arboreal tendencies—she had already broken her leg once in Tahiti by falling out of a mango tree—spent hours aloft on the crosstrees, jumping and chattering like a monkey in a tree when she finally sighted the island lying hazy and mysterious on the horizon. It was late afternoon. The next morning at dawn we closed with the bold forbidding pile under power, for the breeze now was light and dead ahead. When there was light enough to see the shoals we coasted past the base of the precipitous surf-beaten cliffs, and just six days out from Tahiti picked our way through the reefs to anchor off Ahurei village.

2. RAPA

We were anchored in Ahurei Bay in the very heart of the island, surrounded by an almost complete circle of knifelike ridges and two-thousand-foot pinnacles of volcanic rock at the foot of which nestled the village of Ahurei. In spite of the landlocked protection from the sea the anchorage was anything but restful. The whole gloomy island was enveloped in low-hanging clouds from which the mountains seemed to manufacture wind and funnel it down the steep slopes every few minutes in the form of violent williwaws which beat the water to a froth and drove across the bay in a cloud of smokelike spray. In the brief intervals of calm a strong outgoing current would pull the ship broadside to the land. With each blast *Varua* would slew around to face the wind, and our heavy anchor chain would grate and jerk over the uneven bottom. This continued around the clock during the three days we lay there, but we rode to a very long scope and everything held.

"Well anyway," I said, trying to look at the bright side of our distance from shore and the williwaws, "the famous Rapa flies won't bother us." Zizi only laughed.

Just then three whaleboats came alongside, loaded with half the population of Rapa, mainly women and girls. Boats and people were covered with flies and over each boat flew an aerial cover of flies like planes over a carrier. Once alongside, the flies all deserted to *Varua*—apparently their objective all the time. My theory fell apart without further ado. Each night after the last boatload of visitors had gone I wiped out the flies with a bug bomb so we could sleep in peace. Each morning a new detachment ferried out with the first boat.

From aboard, Ahurei village looked romantic in its setting there beneath the precipitous slopes of the dead volcano, in whose crater we were anchored. Ashore the impression changed. An air of shiftlessness lay over everything. The flies were the natural by-product of neglected refuse and bad sanitation. There were some slumlike multiple houses—unknown elsewhere in Oceania. Everything was in disrepair. Even the new dispensary and its attached living quarters were already half deteriorated although still unfinished. There was an electric plant for the radio station —but it did not run—and a partially built and abandoned water supply. Even the growing things seemed sick like the village. The famous Rapa orange trees were everywhere—but they were dead skeletons, killed by a recently introduced blight.

Rapa was obviously the end of the line—the neglected outpost of French Oceania. Most of the schooners of the ridiculous little fleet that brings the produce of the world to the rest of the archipelago avoid Rapa. It is too far; the weather too bad. Rapa learned about World War I after it was over. When a schooner does get here, the voyage has taken so long and the cargo has been so exposed to the elements that much of it arrives spoiled. But nothing stops the blights and diseases.

After one tour of the village and its immediate surroundings the only thing I wanted to do was visit the ancient mountain forts which were visible on the skyline from *Varua* whenever the clouds lifted—perched on the all but inaccessible ridges that circled the bay.

When Vancouver discovered the island in 1791, it was thickly populated with virile clans who waged continual war with each other for possession of the fertile irrigated slopes, and most likely for the sport of the thing as well. I had assumed that the strongholds on the ridges were merely blockhouses defending passes, but now learned that they were actually fortified villages.

The lower slopes were covered with a tangled growth of wild raspberries, like the lantana of Tahiti. The old man who was my guide had to rest frequently as we climbed, and we ate our fill. The last part of the way was up an almost perpendicular goat path which eventually came out on a ridge just wide enough to walk on, with sheer drops on both sides. At the end of the ridge, where it dropped precipitously into the sea, was perched the fort. I was amazed to learn that the "fort" was in reality a complete clan village. The decomposed rock had been leveled off and the little settlement clung there on stone-faced platforms, complete with water catchment basins and taro pits sufficient to withstand long siege. The only approach, along the narrow ridge, had been made quite easy to defend by the simple means of digging a wide, deep trench transversely, its open ends dropping off into nothing and its bottom planted with a thicket of impenetrable brush. Any attackers trying to get past would have been speared like mired pigs while struggling through the ditch. I should imagine, however, that few attacks were made on these strongholds, and that the actual fighting must have consisted of surprise raids on planting parties working the taro beds down on the lower slopes. In any case, a race that could conduct its daily life under such conditions, not to mention waging even limited warfare up there, has my profound respect.

The Rapanese were unique in all Polynesia for these

aerial fortress-villages. They were in those days both virile and numerous. My guide, whose ancestors had been chiefs, said that the records spoke of from four thousand to six thousand inhabitants. When the first native missionaries came to stay in 1826 they estimated over two thousand. The widespread system of ancient stone-bounded taro plantings and irrigation systems, and the extent of the fortified mountain villages, all bear testimony to a large population. But it was the old, old story all over again. The arrival of the first white man, followed shortly afterward by the missionaries, was the beginning of the end. Ironically, on the ship that brought the first apostles of the white man's god came a devastating epidemic, only one of many to follow. To be near the church the people abandoned the healthy, competitive mountain villages and herded together on the unhealthy site at Ahurei, where they were decimated in waves by introduced diseases, wholesale kidnapings by slavers, and the departure of the men to serve at sea. Moerenhout in 1834 found the population down to five hundred. Lieutenant Mery counted a pathetic remnant of one hundred and twenty a generation later, in 1867.

Civilization had not enough to give in return for what it did to Rapa—or perhaps it might be more accurate to say that the benefits came too slowly. The people are no longer dying off; there has even been a slight increase in recent years, to about three hundred when we were there. It was the impact of Western civilization that nearly killed Rapa, but today it is only an intensive application of that very thing that can offer real hope for the future, in an accelerated program of medicine, sanitation, and education, for the past is gone forever.

Rapa itself can be blamed for the fact that the blow was

worse than in the other islands. Its men, like Tino, were too good as sailors. The trading schooners and the whalers called often, and left only more disease in return for the men they took away, until finally it was practically an island of women. Thus developed an intriguing sidelight in the tragic history—the idea of an island run almost exclusively by women. The few men who were left lifted hardly a finger. The women did all the work, from getting firewood to housebuilding, from planting the taro to carrying home the heavy crops on shoulder poles; and from the taro they made endless quantities of *popoi,* the basic food of the island, which was hand-fed to the men, whose fingers had been put under *tapu.* Even today the women manned the sixteen-foot sweeps of the whaleboats that came out to us.

The story of Rapa and its lonely Amazons traveled widely. Unrequited men turned up from far away in America and Europe—until the French government was obliged to call a stop, for this was not the kind of man Rapa wanted. They need not have worried much. The general squalor and unkempt condition of the island and its mistresses would disillusion any but a desperate man. When we were there no white man remained.

The fact that Ahurei village—run almost entirely by women—was the dirtiest, most unsanitary, slumlike settlement in all Polynesia, led to much facetious speculation aboard *Varua* when I questioned the others as to the causes. The theories—none of them very seriously offered—ran from the idea of there being no men to impress and therefore no incentive, to exhaustion from fighting over the few available men, which was Tino's offering.

"Those *vahines* all tired out. Fight too much over men who stay," he laughed, and added something in Tahitian to

Zizi that I could not understand, which brought on Zizi's most unrestrained giggles.

This brought up the subject of wife-beating, a practice not only accepted but even desired by the women of Polynesia. A girl will proudly display a black eye up and down the road, boasting about her man's prowess; while a woman with a gentle husband, lacking the inspiration of an occasional beating, is much more likely to stray from the narrow path. Even Ah You, who expects more subtle means of wife-mastery, saw the point and agreed.

"Look at Reao," she cried, "the only time she is any good is after Remi beats her." This was quite true, Reao being a disorganized but quite beautiful Gauguinish girl who sometimes worked as housegirl for us in Paea.

Perhaps the women of Rapa were too depressed in their unbeaten state to care much about things. Perhaps they were just too tired from doing all the work. In any case the proportion of men to women has been increasing of late. Soon it will be normal. The Amazon psychology still prevails and the women still do all the work. The men have been careful not to encroach upon this prerogative, but pretty soon now I wouldn't be surprised to see things change. Once those Amazons begin to learn about the ideal life their Tahitian sisters lead, the men's sinecure will end. I would like to go back afterward to see if things are more shipshape.

There was little time to explore Rapa thoroughly. When I was ashore I was uneasy, my mind on *Varua* and the williwaws; after two excursions ashore I remained aboard, getting ready for the jumping off. We made a storm cover for the forecastle hatch, which up to then had gone without one. I rechecked everything once more and all I could find to replace was the forestaysail halyard, which for simplification doubled as topsail halyard when that sail was used, by the simple act of unshackling it from the head of the forestaysail and attaching it to the topsail yard. The two sails were never used at the same time. This was the most critical halyard on the ship, for a man's life could depend upon it while working aloft on either of the yards. I felt better starting out with a brand-new one.

We were ready. Why not leave? Our clean laundry was back, brought by an enormous Rapanese woman. She asked for cloth instead of money for her work, nervously polishing the saloon table with the palm of her hand while her fingers curved backward in a typical Rapa gesture. The native medical practitioner had given me two rare stone pestles as well as a beautiful *peue* mat for *Varua,* and would only accept some rope for his cows. Others had asked for kerosene in return for services, for the island was burning candlenuts for light. Rapa had no use for money. They wanted food or goods—and we had no more that we could spare on the eve of our long voyage. They continued to heap largess on us. There was nothing we wanted from Rapa now—it hurt to accept when they had so little. We were ready to go, so why not go?

But this was a special treat for Tino—this visit to his birthplace after twenty-eight years. And for Zizi as well. It would be months before they would see people they could talk with in their own language again. Both Tino and Zizi had spent the two nights so far ashore, appearing somewhat exhausted for work each morning under convoy of a boatload of women. After the first time ashore Zizi—whose store teeth make him look at least ten years younger—left them aboard thereafter in the interests of economy. Perhaps he felt that this was one place where absolutely no effort was required to impress the other sex. I can always tell Zizi's attitude toward whatever port we are in by whether he wears his teeth ashore or not.

On the third day I tentatively wondered if they would mind tearing themselves away soon. They both agreed with surprising alacrity that they were ready to go—that very minute if I wanted.

"Let's call it tomorrow," I told them, "at noon when the light will be best to see the reefs on the way out."

That night when they were rowed ashore by a whaleboat full of Rapa women I thought they displayed a singular lack of enthusiasm.

Before turning in I thumbed through the literature on the Roaring Forties again—Sailing Directions, other voyages —for any previously overlooked clues that might affect our tactics . . . and ended by wishing I had never heard of the books, so full were they of the unpleasant aspect of the region. That is, all except Conor O'Brien, who claimed to have sailed his easting down across the Forties in relative peace and comfort, blaming the usual trepidation with which sailors approach the area on what he called "latitude disease"—a sort of psychosis of fear brought on by the mere fact of being in those dreaded latitudes. But it was not latitude disease that often swept whole watches to their deaths from the driving square-riggers and that battered the ships on pretty nearly every voyage to the point that they lived only to get around the Horn and be done with the region.

Conor O'Brien was a remarkable person. He once spent a week end with me on *Varua* in Gloucester Harbor and I have always remembered his charming personality. He had an instinct for the unusual and may have had a freak spell of fine weather down there that year, but I am more inclined to think that his passage may not have been quite so idyllic as he makes out. He is a master of understatement and there may be a giveaway when he writes: ". . . I say that no adventures are to be found in the Southern Ocean, for it is the most startling thing I can think of to say about it." I think it is likely he was nearer the truth when he wrote on another page that he had ". . . crossed the 50th parallel of latitude, the last stage of the progressive frightfulness with which the Southern Ocean threatens the voyager." In any case, if I may borrow from Conor O'Brien, it is best to confess that I was feeling the early symptoms of latitude disease. The period of incubation is apparently the time it takes to approach the area from a well-known and trusted one.

I put the books away on their shelves behind their rolling bar and went on deck to look at the night before turning in. A full moon broke into the clear from behind fast clouds from time to time and shone on the peaks of the ancient volcano rim. The gusts hurled themselves down the steep slopes onto the rather grandly beautiful bay and there was a bite of cold in the wind that I had not felt for a long time. *Varua* gave to the first force of each squall with an easy roll; her anchor chain grated and brought up taut. Rapa was a lonely last outpost—already well out of the voluptuous tropical Pacific I knew so well. For a moment I thought how nice it would be to swing over to Mangareva from here, then north through the Paumotus and back to Tahiti. What did we want with the Roaring Forties after all, and wind-tormented, rainy southern Chile? How much easier to make the trip by steamer from Panama! There were even planes flying on schedule to Punta Arenas these days. I shivered a little from a particularly heavy williwaw and went below.

The next day for a final morale booster I sent everybody ashore to bathe in the scanty stream. The "rivers" Tino and Zizi had reassured Ah You about had turned out to be anything but that—but water trickling over stones, no matter how scanty, was better than no stream at all. I preferred my efficient shower aboard *Varua*. While they were gone I saw to the topping off of our tanks with water brought out by whaleboats in five-gallon tins, so that we could start our long voyage with everything full to overflowing.

From on shore I could hear the peculiar hollow booming of the *popoi* beaters. Taro is the usual ingredient, but other starchy fruits and vegetables can also be used, and since I had found that our large supply of bananas from Ofaipapa were ripening too fast I had sent them in to be converted into *popoi:* the strange, sour, pudding-like substance that would keep indefinitely. Anyone in Rapa would have known from the sound of the pounding, even at this distance, exactly who was making our *popoi*—for the stone beaters are prized not only for weight and texture but for tone as well. To me it was an impersonal but nostalgic sound that I would forever associate with Rapa.

Our crew came back—happy as only Tahitians can be after a bath in a stream—Ah You and Piho with flowers in their freshly washed hair and fern wreaths on their heads, Tino and Zizi surrounded by so many women I could see only the tops of their heads as they stood in the whaleboat. They were loaded with presents—invariably produce of the island—plus our *popoi*. The other two whaleboats convoyed them, equally laden. Once again we searched *Varua* for things we could spare from our precious stores as return gifts. There was almost nothing, but by sheer chance someone thought of ice water, which proved to be the hit of our stay. Young and old, everyone in the three whaleboats, all jostled laughingly to get their glass of ice water—and thus went the last of our Tahiti ice.

The clinking pitchers were passed around, overhead because the crowd was too thick; glasses were filled and refilled and passed from hand to hand—to all who were able to crowd aboard and to the standees in the whaleboats alongside—until finally there was no more ice, and *Varua*'s water supply had been reduced by so many gallons that I sent a whaleboat ashore a last time to fill up the five-gallon cans again.

Two of the Rapa men stayed to help crank the windlass to get in the seventy-five fathoms of chain and our heaviest anchor—but they were so water-logged they could do little more than perspire streams on the deck while Tino and Zizi practically swung them around on the winch handles.

To our amused eyes the boats seemed much lower in the water than before. As we moved slowly away the village shore took on its original aspect of romance and hospitality and we forgot the squalor. It wasn't much of a place and it hadn't made much of an impression on any of us. It was neither tropical nor temperate. There were a hundred islands more spectacular. There was even nothing about the people that appealed very much to us, but the crowd in the whaleboats seemed suddenly very dear to us, for where we were going it was cold and inhospitable, and these were the last people we would see for a long time.

3. THE GREAT SOUTHERN SEA

It was noon January 11 when I conned the ship out through the reefs that block the entrance to Ahurei Bay. From the vantage point of the topsail yard *Varua* looked long and slender—almost fragile to be setting out on such a voyage. Her strength lay in her careful design and in her beauty, not in massive construction. An hour later we were safely clear of the land and its hazards, sailing south close-hauled to a light southeasterly breeze. A sailing ship silently leaving the shelter of port, depending on the winds to drive her thousands of miles across the sea to a distant land, is always a thing of beauty and romance. As the island drew astern, the vastness of the sea ahead took on for a moment an almost tangible quality. Reluctantly I came down to make the first small mark on the chart—the beginning of the faint penciled track that was to extend itself, at a pace infinite in its slowness, across the empty wastes of the great southern ocean.

We were off on the real thing now—no more interludes, no respite until Chile. We were to sail some thousand miles south through the variables until reaching the westerlies, somewhere below the fortieth parallel. Then we would turn eastward and run for three thousand miles—"the great wind roaring fresh behind us and the seas breaking high"—with only the far-ranging albatross for company: the climax of my years of ocean sailing. The next land we would see would be the southern coast of Chile, down near the Patagonian channels.

For too many years now I had sailed *Varua* in dependable trade wind regions, counting on her sleek easily driven hull to do her one hundred and fifty miles a day or better. This was to be the fastest passage ever. We would average our modest one hundred and fifty getting south. Then, once in the Roaring Forties, we would run as we had never run before. We would cover those last three thousand miles in not much over two weeks. *Varua* had been designed for this very thing—to run safely before big following seas. With luck, I hoped, we would see the coast of Chile three weeks after leaving Rapa. I actually thought we could do it.

I should have known better. One does not go on sailing voyages on schedule. The one sea superstition I really believe in is never to predict fast passages. It is fatal. I knew that the westerlies had been known to fail other ships—for instance the voyage of the *Grace Harwar* with Alan Villiers in the 1929 Grain Race—but cases like this were rare. Findlay says: "In this region easterly winds are very rare and only of brief duration." Certainly it would not happen to us. I should have known better.

That first day, sailing south from Rapa, and that first night, slipping along at six knots under a full moon, only a slight heel and the hiss of water past the hull revealed the fact that we were in motion. I wondered how I could have been so craven a few days ago as to harbor the temptation to give up the voyage and sail back via Mangareva. Only the long powerful swell coming up from the south reminded us that all would not remain so peaceful.

I had always been curious about the night sky down there, about the stars we would steer by when the Southern Cross was too high in the heavens. But the southern sky was a disappointment, with almost nothing to replace the old favorites that faded astern in the north.

That night was one of the few occasions when we were to be privileged to see the sky at all, day or night, for the following morning ushered in the gray rainy weather and head winds we were to know so well. As the heavy overcast blotted out the blue sky the two girls took off their wide-brimmed pandanus hats and sadly put them away. Later, in the cold and wet of the far south, they would ask me from time to time when they could wear their Happy Hats again. To overcome the heavy weight of homesickness they engaged in the first of the many lengthy Tahiti Admiration Society sessions which became a feature of life aboard *Varua*. With the unrestrained imaginations of Tahitians they would discuss in great detail the various desirable phases of life in Tahiti, sometimes by themselves, sometimes with all of us joining in. One day it would be fruits—going over one by one all the known fruits of Tahiti, savoring mentally the joys of gathering them, their relative sweetness and sourness. Another day it would be seafoods, or the reef and everything that lived on it, or the valley. Shut in on the most strenuous days, they could create for themselves a living atmosphere of their beloved island and be absolutely oblivious to the cold desolate surroundings. I often envied them their faculty, as I struggled into woolens and oilskins to take the wheel on a freezing wet night.

In the tropics Tino's years of experience qualified him to make or reduce sail on his own during my watch below, but, like myself, Tino had never seen this new kind of world and did not know what to expect of it. So from then on I was on call twenty-four hours a day, although the thud of seas, the changed tempo of vibration in the rigging, or sheer instinct usually brought me on deck before the men called.

THE GREAT SOUTHERN SEA

Our daytime watches were fairly flexible, adjusted to give each of us the chance to do our respective tasks and get a three-hour rest sometime during the day. At night we three men stood three-hour wheel watches, alone on deck except in unusual circumstances. Each of us had one six-hour stretch in which to get a good sleep. We did not shift watches every day as is usually done, for I believe it is more restful to get used to certain hours and stick to them. The two girls took the wheel at odd times during the day in most weather, although Ah You was too seasick for this when the going got really rough. She always managed to keep things shipshape below. Piho was never sick and became a valuable extra helmsman, often taking an early evening or morning watch to let one of us catch up on lost sleep.

On most voyages with normal weather, nothing is more enjoyable than the tranquillity of a spell at the wheel, reading a good book or daydreaming. This trip, with its extremes of cold and wet and the gray colorlessness and monotony of bad weather, turned out to be another story. Toward the end we all longed to be able to spend the whole night in a warm stationary berth.

With the south wind on the second day came also the first indication of the penetrating cold which was to be our greatest bugbear. We began the cumbersome business of putting on woolens and wearing oilskins and boots for warmth even when it was not wet on deck. Neither of the girls had ever had anything heavier than thin cotton on them before, and my efforts to get them into and keep them in suitable costume were amusing and sometimes pathetic. They seemed happier shivering with a thin *pareu* clutched around them than warmly bundled up in my woolen pants and L. L. Bean shirts. They also wanted to keep bathing on deck in the rain and in cold that had the three hardy male seafarers congealed. Finally I, as master, thinking of pneumonia and probably subconsciously of our male pride, ordered them to desist until we again reached warmer regions. We had plenty of warm water for them to bathe in, within reason, down below.

So on the second day, the sleeping giant stirred; the ominous swell from the south mounted and heavy squalls in the night forced us to reduce sail. The barometer began strange gyrations which were to keep me in suspense for most of the voyage. And on the third day shortly after daybreak—so soon—we were reduced to two staysails, hove to in our first gale. It came straight from the south, where we wanted to go.

As we got *Varua* snugged down and sailing herself slowly along through a quickly rising sea, a steamer emerged from the rain curtain about a mile off and steamed stolidly on her course to the southwest, taking heavy spray over her bridge. We had not realized how big the seas were until we saw the steamer disappear to her flying bridge each time she was in the trough. She crossed our stern a half-mile or so away and disappeared in the rain, heading for New Zealand or Australia, from Panama—the only route as far south as this—having paid not the slightest attention to the small white brigantine hove to there in the rising gale. Although we had shown our flag, she had not. We wondered under what flag efficiency had come to the point where a steamer would not turn a few degrees off her course to hail a lonely sailing ship far off the beaten path in the southern ocean. We saw no more ships. From then on we were south of the region where ships go today. We were alone in the world of gray driving rain, gray sky, and gray seas.

✦

THE GREAT SOUTHERN SEA

It was just a modest little gale. *Varua* and the elements, the two opponents, felt one another out, sparring for time and waiting. At noon the rolling gray seas were breaking heavily enough to be dangerous and we went into strategic retreat for a few hours, running off before the worst of the seas, working as much east as possible in between. By coincidence the course we averaged led in the direction of our old temptation, Mangareva, still only about six hundred miles to the northeast. The wind was bitterly cold and the rain stung like hail. The crests hung menacingly over our stern and flung us away from the direction in which we ought to be sailing. Poor Ah You was desperately seasick. I was tempted to put the foresail on and let *Varua* drive. In four days we could be in Mangareva where it was warm and the sea was blue.

Setbacks in the first few days are always discouraging; doubly so this trip for I was really intimidated. I wanted to make the voyage more than almost anything, but doubt gripped me recurringly. I had read too much. I remembered too well all those sailors' stories of the great gales and seas and tragedies of the Roaring Forties. It was all very romantic to want to experience it too, in theory; but in practice, confronted by the real thing, I was not so sure. Perhaps the moral is: Don't read—stick to the pilot chart for your technical information, and let it go at that.

For eight hours we drove on in the direction of Mangareva. I took the wheel as night fell and sent the men below. *Varua* worked beautifully and bested the seas easily. After a little while I could see the barometer in the chartroom moving up again. I thought I felt a softening in the drive of the wind and seas and knew instinctively we could carry sail again. My hand reached for the bellpull beside the wheel, and Zizi and Tino appeared through the dark, whistling from the cold bite of the wind and furling their *pareus* to keep from losing them.

"Jib," I shouted at them, with upward gesture. They disappeared in the dark forward and I steered with care to keep the wind just over the starboard quarter. A trembling through the ship told me the sail was going up. When it was up the trembling stopped and I could feel the weight of it. The men appeared again, streaming with the rain, bodies gleaming in the dim light from the binnacle port.

"Jib okay," Tino shouted.

"Mainsail up. Careful now."

The sail was already reefed. Zizi was at the halyard winch with Tino controlling the leech and boom lift. We were still running off. I steered with one hand and slacked the mainsheet with the other as Tino set up the boom guy. The sail pressed heavily against mast and shrouds but went up all right. *Varua* picked up speed, riding the crests for an appreciable time. Just as one had passed I spun the wheel hard and the men sheeted in fast. When the following sea broke *Varua* was well around, taking it on her starboard bow in a smother of phosphorescence. Lightly she lifted with it, taking only broken water on deck—and slowly forged ahead into the night, close-hauled. She was no longer in retreat. Mangareva was astern. It was our turn to attack.

For days we drove against a persistent southeast wind, working south through the Thirties. We rarely saw the sun. When we did—usually very briefly around midday—it was always surrounded by either a rainbow or a halo. The weather book said that:

Cirrostratus, a sheet of high thin cloud, gives the sky a milky appearance, through which the sun or moon may shine, producing a halo. Cirrostratus should be watched for if it grows lower and seems to thicken, it is usually a sign of the approach of a weather disturbance. . . .

I never took much stock in such signs but now began to keep a record of halos and barometer gymnastics, hoping to make some order out of it all. I gave up when I found that the sun never appeared without its halo, and the resulting weather made no sense at all: sometimes good, sometimes bad. The cold increased and our old friend the big southerly swell continued to hold forth. The moon was seen only as a ghost slipping furtively across a thin place in the overcast.

At 3:30 A.M. on January 16, on an extremely high barometer, we were again down to the two lower staysails with a moderate gale from east-southeast; which was all right, for we lashed the wheel and left *Varua* to work her way south on her own while we caught up on sleep. She forged ahead slowly but steadily, although a heavy cross-sea made the motion fairly bad. Ah You, who had begun to feel better, shook her head sorrowfully.

"Aué!" she protested. "Ça commence encore." And she resignedly took to her berth again.

Slept out, I reread *The Moon and Sixpence* to the steady moan of wind and the rush of rain water on deck. An occasional big sea broke close alongside with a roar and a thud.

I had never expected anything but an easy passage south through the Thirties. This was Roaring Forty weather—but from the wrong direction. From what we saw of these latitudes they deserve to be called the Dirty Thirties.

Twenty-eight hours later—tempted by comfort and security to remain hove to, but remembering how often one wastes hours of good wind once a gale starts to ease up—we tried more sail and soon had her under four lowers, heading slightly west of south. The sun appeared with its halo just long enough for me to get a noon sight. We had made about eighty miles in twenty-eight hours while hove to under two small staysails. Now we were flying.

Later we added the big No. 2 and No. 3 upper staysails. It was really too soon for No. 3, but since I was beginning to look for a gale lurking behind each movement of the barometer it seemed necessary to make some gesture of defiance. The sail held, surprisingly, and we drove on with exhilarating speed into the south, over long impressive swells that rolled up now from the southwest. But the wind was still from the east.

Just before dusk came an outrider from the cold latitudes ahead—our first albatross, soaring down from the pale overcast in motionless majestic flight to sweep past us in a steep bank.

"Aieee!" cried Tino, who like all of us had never seen the king of sea birds before. "Better than Air Tahiti!" And at first glance the giant bird did look comparable to the small plane which had recently started interisland service in Tahiti. From now on the albatross were to be our daily companions, increasing in numbers as we worked south, helping to keep up morale in the face of discouragements.

The night was cold and crisp. We caught a glimpse of the old moon, in its last quarter now. I was reminded of New England—even to the drop on the end of the nose.

The next day our wake still swept astern recklessly. I subtracted mile after mile from the remaining distance to the Forties, and the turning point east. With the facility of all sailors I forgot overnight the discouragement of the first few days, avidly rereading the very material I had then shuddered to think of. There was reassurance in Findlay: "These westerly winds blow with a constancy almost equal to the Trade Winds." He calls them the "Anti-Trades" or "Passage

Winds." Maury waxed eloquent when he came to describe the "Brave West Winds":

> To appreciate the force and volume of these polarbound winds in the southern hemisphere, it is necessary that one should "run them down" in that waste of water beyond the parallel of 40° S, where "the winds howl and the seas roar." The billows there lift themselves up in long ridges with deep hollows between them. They run high and fast, tossing their white caps aloft in the air, looking like the green hills of a rolling prairie capped with snow, and chasing each other in sport. Still their march is stately and their roll majestic.

The ship, Maury promised, would find herself "followed for weeks at a time by these magnificent rolling swells, driven and lashed by the 'brave west winds' furiously."

I traced our proposed route on the pilot chart. We would go just far enough within the Forties to get the edge of the westerly gales and the favorable current. Then, running east, we would stay well below Forty until around 120° West Longitude where we would swing up to the thirty-eighth or thirty-ninth parallel to avoid the too-frequent gales below Forty. This would also keep us in a warmer isotherm. Nearing the coast, we would swing south to forty again to reach Valdivia, an important town upriver from Corral, southernmost Pacific port of Chile. It was a conservative plan—staying within the belt of westerlies the whole way but avoiding the more severe gales and cold farther south.

With the smooth motion and the enthusiasm of the day, I decreed hot baths and hair washing for everyone. Cabin windows steamed up. Tropical clothes were stowed away and we took stock of our heavy weather things, for we were nearing Forty and the westerlies might begin any moment now.

The wind died out in the southeast. We sailed into a region of squalls with calms in between. Beyond this doldrum area would surely lie waiting our Brave West Wind. Forty was only a day's run south now. The squalls rained themselves out. *Varua* rolled listlessly, sails slatting. All impatient, I started the engine and we rolled south with everything furled. There was not a breath of wind but the swell was still there. Even the barograph indicated a change in the weather, going along on a straight line instead of rising and falling with its usual daily rhythm. Something was surely going on in the Forties.

When one has talked so much of getting down to the fortieth parallel and the westerlies one half expects to find a signpost there—TURN LEFT, CHILE 3000 MILES—plus a westerly wind all tuned up and blowing fresh. In any case, I felt that once over the invisible line, with anything slightly resembling a favorable wind, we would be on the homestretch. There was, of course, the matter of three thousand miles still to go, but temporarily at any rate I had been conditioned in my thinking to look forward with relief to three thousand miles of supposedly fair-wind sailing, gales and all, after plugging close-hauled into head winds for two thousand miles.

It was January 21. We were ten days out from Rapa. At midnight we had crossed into the Promised Land, and, sure enough, we had a new wind which had come in with a bang. We were shortened down to working sails, driving hard—not gloriously, not even enthusiastically, for the new wind was from the *east!* And, curiously enough, that long ominous southwest swell that had been baiting us for days petered out and was replaced by increasingly disagreeable cross-seas from several directions. Thus did the Roaring Forties receive us.

By keeping *Varua* close-hauled and driving hard we could make about southeast now, which helped some but brought us each day into colder weather, for which we were poorly prepared. But we let her drive, confident the easterly couldn't last. With the ship's head pointed even slightly toward Chile there was a mounting of spirit aboard, a burst of singing and banter. Tino and Zizi became so engrossed in exchanging nonsense about Chilean women that they forgot to take their watch below. Another big Tahitian, named Upa, who had sailed with me to Honolulu, had brought back from there a *popaa* wife, in spite of the fact that he already had a Tahitian *vahine* at home, all of which had led to certain complications on his return. Tino and Zizi also had wives at home but swore they were not going to be outdone by Upa. Later, on the basis that we had reached an important milestone in our voyage even if we did have a head wind, Zizi went below and concocted a reasonably good Tahitian feast out of the most unlikely ingredients. The only legitimate things in it were the *popoi* from Rapa and coconut in several forms from the large supply of nuts under the forecastle floor.

The thermometer so far had only admitted to a low of 55° Fahrenheit, but with driving rain and spray and the cold sea under us it seemed much worse. The special tropical arrangements of *Varua* were liabilities now. From the tenth day on, the Aladdin gimbal lamp was kept burning steadily day and night to warm the saloon. Shortly afterward, the two-burner Primus stove was lashed to our swinging table for additional heat. The Primus had been aboard for years as insurance against trouble with our Shipmate diesel range, but had never before been used. Both the Aladdin and the Primus were still burning when we reached Chile; in fact, they kept burning until we were north of Valparaiso. I will never again hear the fluttering hum of a

Primus stove without thinking of those cold days down in the southern ocean.

As we drove on south and the cold increased, Ah You made heavy flannel mittens, and scuffs to wear in our sea boots. When we found we were still cold on watch we took to wearing two suits of oilskins, one over the other, on top of woolen clothes. Almost always it was raining. When the rain stopped we still had a form of precipitation, unexpected to say the least. The sails had all been treated with water-repellent mildew-proof solution, which now caused them to perspire so heavily in the cold damp air that streams of condensation ran from them.

So we stood on across the Roaring Forties, but with the wind from the east instead of the west. Every day we were farther south, and colder, but convinced that somewhere down there the westerly gales must be blowing and that if we just kept on we would reach them eventually.

The cold black nights were plagued by squalls but so far they had not been dangerous. One night we were caught. I had taken my usual evening wheel, from supper to 9 P.M. Scenting trouble, I carried on into Zizi's watch. There were several squalls but they turned out to be mostly rain with little wind, so at eleven o'clock I called Zizi and turned in. A half hour later I awoke to a real one. Without waiting to put on clothes I spun the wheel and we ran before it while Zizi and Tino got No. 2 and No. 3 staysails down.

We often carry these light staysails under conditions that would normally be unsafe—except for the fact that they are so light and cheap that they would blow out before endangering ship or rig. I consider them semiexpendable. If damaged, they are easy to repair. Even the cost of replacement is negligible, for we make them ourselves. If we get caught, they come down in a flash, brailed against the mast by the downhaul. Later Tino can go aloft at leisure and make a neat furl, unless the squall is short-lived, in which case we reset them from the deck.

When we have carried these light sails too long the trick is to blanket them with the mainsail as they are hauled down. To accomplish this it is only necessary to bring the wind astern for about thirty seconds. But this time a violent shift at the critical instant caught us off balance. The men had the two staysails safely brailed in but the wind got behind the mainsail during one heavy roll just long enough for it to flog once with a noise like a thunderclap. The boom guy prevented serious consequences. Not until Tino called me at dawn did we see what had happened. The head of the mainsail was torn almost off, two feet under the tabling. The fact that we always carry the weight of the boom on the lift, plus the pressure of wind holding the sail against mast and shrouds, had prevented it from coming down during the night. Had I been completely alert, instead of just coming out of a heavy sleep into a wild night, it probably would not have torn at this time, although it would have happened sooner or later, for I discovered that in my inspection for possible sources of trouble I had overlooked one thing. Shackles of a new type that I had installed in Tahiti, to attach the mainsail to the mast slides, had been chafing the luff rope of the sail. At one point near the head of the sail the rope had been cut almost through, and when the extra strain had come it had parted. We got out the palms and needles and soon had the sail repaired. Before setting it again we seized rings to the luff rope and passed the shackles through them, eliminating the possibility of further chafe. Once again the ship was whole, and had her guard up.

We passed the forty-fifth parallel, the absolute farthest south I had ever contemplated going. Still it blew half a gale from the east. Some strange fate was guiding us remorselessly along the blue line on the pilot chart that represented the sailing route from Tahiti to Cape Horn. Day after day found us following the blue line, and it began to be obvious that under existing circumstances it would be easier to go around the Horn than to reach Valdivia. Much as this might have tempted me any other time, there were urgent reasons why we could not do it this trip. The most important was an addition to the crew which Ah You was promising us. For various sentimental reasons I wanted this event to occur in Panama. There was time for a little of Patagonia, the Humboldt Current, and the West Coast—but not for Cape Horn, for that would mean circumnavigating South America.

On January 25 we were in 46° South Latitude approaching the broken red line on the pilot chart that indicated the northern limit of the region where icebergs have been encountered at this season. That evening we had a spine-chilling experience. I think we sailed directly over an uncharted shoal, although even today I am uncertain about it. We were under full sail with a fresh breeze, doing about seven knots. I was at the wheel when I suddenly noticed discolored water around the ship. Leaping to my feet I saw what looked exactly like bottom, not more than six or eight fathoms down, extending unbroken as far as I could see in all directions. Mottled yellowish brown and light green in color, it raced past beneath our keel, threatening full disaster.

A heavy line squall with its slanting gray rain curtain was rapidly approaching from the north. Sounding leads were stowed away somewhere below. There was an instant only

THE GREAT SOUTHERN SEA

of hesitation—a choice between the scientific urge to verify a discovery and responsibility for the ship and the lives of those aboard. There might be shallower areas on which we would strike. It would soon be dark. The only thing was to get away as fast and as far as possible while daylight lasted.

Within twenty seconds I was on the crosstrees, with Tino on my heels. Ah You rushed up on deck in response to my shouts to take the wheel. Tino and I stayed up there looking for signs of breakers until it was dark. The shoal, if it was one, was considerably more than a mile across, for we were over it at least ten minutes, sailing seven knots. To us on the mast it seemed hours before the ugly menace beneath us receded and we were once again riding over the usual gray-green void.

If it was not a shoal, it must have been some kind of marine organism. It could not have been a reflection of clouds because by chance the sky was clear at the time—so rare a condition that I noted the fact in the log. This was in 46° South Latitude and 128° West Longitude. The nearest sounding on the chart, just one, showed 2,440 fathoms about thirty miles to the west-northwest. There were no other soundings recorded within about two hundred miles.

That same night we entered the region where icebergs might be encountered, feeling like Antarctic explorers. Tino and Zizi, whose iceberg education had been somewhat neglected, looked at me curiously as I described the hazard which now confronted us and for which we would from now on keep constant lookout. The only ice they had seen came from Martin's *Brasserie* in Papeete and came in one-hundred-pound blocks, which was a far cry from the island as big as Mehetia made all of ice which I described to them, having just read up on the subject myself. Islands of ice in the abstract were pretty hard for them to take, but as soon as I showed them a picture in the *National Geographic* of an ice floe in Baffin Bay with a polar bear on it they were convinced. The improbability of the thing was removed by the presence of the bear.

There was a great deal of joking about finding an iceberg with a good harbor so we could go ashore and bathe in a river, and so on. The inability of Tahitians to take any situation seriously was a good thing just then, because I was worried. It was the Antarctic summer and the melting icebergs would be drifting far to the north, possibly as far as the region we were then crossing. About the only point in our favor was that the nights were short. But they were also black, and the mere fact of being where we were made them seem colder and more unfriendly than ever before.

There had been another bad moment of temptation when I realized that the wind was settling back into the northeast and building up to gale force. This meant that we must either keep heading deeper into the dangerous area, still hoping for our west wind, or turn and go on the starboard tack. In the latter case we would be heading back where we came from, where it was warm and seductive. For a while I actually considered giving up and sailing directly back to the islands. It would have been the easiest thing in the world, for although I felt completely cured of Latitude Disease, we all had Tahiti Disease. From the first day out we had been planning what we would do when we returned. We could get all cheered up at the drop of a hat discussing Tahiti. But temptation whispered in vain, for this had become a personal thing now between myself and the elements. All my combined Scotch-Swiss ancestral obstinacy was aroused. We would fight it and lick it if we had to beat

THE GREAT SOUTHERN SEA

all the way to Valdivia, which was still nearly three thousand miles dead to windward. We would stay on this tack if necessary to Fifty South. It was unthinkable that the easterly could be blowing in Fifty South. We were probably on the wrong side of a high pressure ridge. A hundred miles might bring us into winds of opposite direction. If the easterly was still blowing below the fiftieth parallel we would turn back and keep plugging until the inevitable break came.

The barometer was very unsteady, trending downward. There were clouds racing from several directions. The wind roses on the pilot chart recorded no easterly winds whatsoever in this vicinity. From hour to hour we expected the shift to come. I plotted a new, combined Great Circle–Mercator course which would take us back outside the ice limit and skirt just to the north of it, and eventually bring us to Valdivia. All night we waited for the shift to come.

But next day, instead of changing, it was blowing a gale from the northeast; and we were hove to, driving still farther to the southeast, still uncannily following the Tahiti–Cape Horn track on the chart, still determined to keep on until we found the westerlies.

There had been a whale under our stern after dawn. My notoriously acute nose had detected it the day before and during the night, to everyone's amusement and disbelief. Happily I was able to present it to the others almost at arm's length. There were more albatross than we had ever seen, soaring down the valleys between the seas, lifting without a flicker of their great wings to clear the breaking crests miraculously. And with the increasing power of the gale came increasing cold—in the forties at night, barely 50° F. by day. We saw our breath congealing white in the gray dawn. Piho came up unforewarned and stood by me in the well.

"Something is making me smoke inside," she cried, watching her breath with fascinated horror.

The cold was really serious—actually the only critical aspect, for we had plenty of stores and water to fight the thing through. What we did not have was proper clothes for an extended cold-weather voyage. Our makeshift mitts got wet all the time. Even the two suits of oilskins were not enough to protect us through a three-hour watch. The galley was steaming with drying things at all hours. I thought of the real Cape Horners whose crews had no warm galley to dry out in—only a cold flooded-out forecastle where everything stayed wet until they had rounded the Horn and finally reached the trade winds again. By comparison we had all the comforts imaginable—except that three-hour watch at night, which was pretty bad.

Varua was steering herself now, driving against the continuing gale under the two storm staysails. The man on ice watch had only to stand in the charthouse companionway with head and shoulders out. So, to cheer us all up, we gathered there and had a very heavy Tahiti Admiration Society talk, complete with our portable Primus stove to take the chill off, planning for the hundredth time what we would do when we got back.

The gale began on January 26 and lasted four days. It never shifted in the slightest but blew with unabated force day and night from approximately northeast. And I am not taking the term "gale" lightly. It should be sufficient to say that under the two small storm staysails (fore and main) we were forging through heavy seas slightly to windward, with wheel lashed, and making better than a hundred miles a day. The first day was probably moderate gale force. On the second and part of the third day it was without doubt full gale. At noon on the second day the sun appeared momentarily with its halo and I was able to get our latitude. We were in 49° S. I almost felt that I had dreamed up the whole business about the "westerlies."

On the third day, with the gale still blowing relentlessly from the same direction, we crossed the fiftieth parallel. We were three hundred miles inside the region where ice might be encountered. Obstinacy can become folly if persisted in too long. We were convinced that there were no fair winds in the southern ocean anywhere, and we had had enough. A few hours later, picking our chance, we wore around onto the starboard tack and headed back in the direction from which we had come.

January 28, when we reached our farthest south and turned back, was Ah You's birthday. We had expected to be approaching the coast of Chile by now instead of marking time under two scraps of storm canvas in 50° S., midway along the Cape Horn route. I had been apologizing to her for the unlikely easterly gales which had brought us to such a place.

"I am thinking of Faaone," she told me, as we watched the driving seas blot out the cabin windows at regular intervals. Viewed from beneath the surface the sea was green. Whenever the rectangle of thick glass cleared itself momentarily we had a glimpse of a heaving arc of sullen gray sky. She thoughtfully refrained from comparing the wild scene with other birthdays in the warm peaceful valley she had loved.

For days now she had not left the familiar cabin with its color and security and grudging warmth. Her courage was still strong but the body was weak from continued seasickness. Even though the wind and sea were the worst we had yet seen and the barometer was falling steeply as we recrossed the fiftieth parallel, the fact that we were heading again toward warmer and supposedly kindlier latitudes was the best present she could have had.

For almost three thousand miles now we had fought close-hauled, gaining easting most of the time but reaching far into the cold southern latitudes to do it. Now, retreating from the cold, we were giving up part of that precious easting. It was a far cry from the two hundred miles a day we had expected to be running off before the westerlies. The heavy monotonous grayness, which would have been exciting as a setting for a wild racing voyage, created an almost unbearable oppression when combined with unceasing head winds.

The only thing that could be said for our new course was that it relieved to a certain extent the worry about ice. We had been over that ground and had seen nothing. Nevertheless the hazard was always there, and the standard instruction to the helmsman continued to be "Watch for ice!"

The nights were in reality short. But the cold groping hours that began when I came down from the masthead after a last straining look around just before the dark closed in seemed an eternity. I breathed freely again only when dawn came and we could see once more.

By noon the following day we were back where we had been two days previously. The gale was blowing itself out in the northeast. Soon we had the reefed mainsail and jib on her and were obliged to leave our somewhat warm retreats below in order to start steering once more. There seemed no end to the cold steady rain. The best course we could make against the high sea that was still running had us headed somewhere between Rapa, which we had left eighteen days before, and Mangareva. Mangareva was now almost two thousand miles distant.

I was worried about Ah You's continued seasickness, and beginning to wonder if, after all, we did have enough stores to fight easterly gales much longer.

It was one of the rare times in years of voyaging that I felt an almost unmanageable depression. Part of it was no doubt due to the mass of clothing we were obliged to wear. Struggling into layer after layer following a quick shuddering sponge bath in the unheated bathroom, I would think of the pool by the waterfall in my stream in Tahiti, and the *pareu* which would be my solitary garment after a leisurely swim—and I would wonder why I had ever left my beloved tropics.

That evening the wind drifted uncertainly around through north, having blown from east and northeast with varying force, mostly gale, for ten days. To our indescribable joy it fell calm. The seas turned into swift moving rollers without crests. By all signs and the law of averages as well, this was surely the end of our head winds: the calm before the return of the truant westerlies. Without the wind the cold lost its bite. Even the persistent drizzle was bearable.

The radio brought us Spanish music from South America, the first contact with our supposed destination. Tino, who had been sleeping on the transom in the chartroom to be close at hand during the worst days of the gale, moved back to the forecastle. The two girls cheered up to the extent of washing their hair. Ah You's was below her hips now. As they combed for each other, they chattered about what it would be like when we reached the island. Nothing I said would ever change their conception of the world as a collection of islands. Some, like France and America, were only bigger than others. With the calm came the first silence we had experienced since being in albatross latitudes. We heard for the first time the sound made by the great birds as they soared close alongside in the gathering dusk. It was like the whistling hiss of a plane coming in to land with motors cut. There were only one or two left and they soon disappeared. The albatross likes the gale, not the calm.

Relaxed by the unaccustomed calm we slept peacefully that night waiting for a new wind. *Varua*, with wings folded, found her way confidently over the long sweeping rollers left over from the gales.

At 1 A.M. Tino called me to announce with a big bristly grin that there was a new wind—from the south. The joy and excitement was so great that all hands threw on oilskins and hurried on deck into the wet blackness of the night to help. Soon *Varua* was under full fore and aft sail— even to the old expendables, No. 2 and No. 3 staysails. At long last we were forging ahead on a course of our own choosing.

The luxury of being able to steer toward our destination lasted three hours. When I came up at 4 A.M. to take the wheel it was blowing hard. Soon the upper staysails had to come off. By the time Tino came down from passing the gaskets, the wind had shifted—not to the west as hoped, but to southeast. Soon we were down to reefed lowers. The old northeast sea built up again, with the new sea commencing to break over it. Day brought only a dismal solid overcast, a cold steady drizzle. We were headed, for a change, toward northern Peru instead of southern Chile.

Even though it was another bitter disappointment, we were at least on a course which would bring us out of the iceberg region and allow us to gain easting as well. But I think

THE GREAT SOUTHERN SEA

from this point on I was ready to accept the idea that the books and pilot charts were all wrong. There *were* no prevailing westerlies. Even the law of averages did not apply down here. Just winds from easterly quadrants.

Another twenty-four hours passed, and it was the last day of January. Miraculously I found the sun in the sextant telescope through a momentary break in the clouds at noon and found it again a couple of hours later to give us an accurate fix—which to my astonishment was only five miles out from our dead reckoning after three days without sights—three days of very tough going, on various courses, often with no one at the wheel.

By nightfall it was colder than ever, the southeast wind fresh from the Antarctic. I was cold on my first night watch, so when I came up later I put on three pairs of pants and three shirts and on top of them the infallible oilskins and boots. Again I cursed the absolute boredom of getting into and out of so many clothes so often, and dreamed at the wheel of the long soft tropic watches we had kept in warmer latitudes, nodding sleepily but contentedly through the hours. There was no tendency to fall asleep at the wheel these nights. We were too busy pounding warmth into our extremities, learning new tricks with the neck towel to keep out the driving fine rain or the occasional heavy dousing from a lurcher. Strangely enough, cold as we were, often wet through and obliged to sit out our watch that way, we had no colds, no chills, no aftereffects.

When day came on the first of February the cold vanished and we had our only warm day since the departure from Rapa. It was not the balmy warmth of our tropics—only 58° F. at noon—but it was enough, and we were starting on our last two thousand miles. The girls got out their Happy Hats for a little while and gave their morale an immense boost. This day was referred to for the rest of the voyage as the Warm Day—the only day we went without layers of clothes and oilskins. I wrote in the logbook at noon that unless the wind went ahead again we could get out of the iceberg region by midnight.

The wind fell to a light breeze, working into the south, while for the first time during the voyage we spread our squaresails, gambling that finally the law of averages was about to operate and produce fair winds. And sure enough, in the middle of the afternoon the breeze began to waver, a swell came from the west, the sea became confused and jerky and the glass began to fall again, steadily. The next round was coming up.

The sun set dramatically, a fiery red disc on the horizon under a low cloud bank. For a few hours the stars shone from a clear sky. We saw the moon for the second time, and the dying breeze moved slowly past south and on around to west as we drifted through the night watches. Day dawned, and with it came the fresh northwest wind we had hoped for so long.

It was our first wind from a westerly quadrant since leaving Tahiti. At last we steered in the direction we wanted to go, with sheets eased, our square foresail and topsail adding the immense power of their lifting pull to the reaching drive of the other sails.

For days now I had been struggling to throw off the tense feeling that I could by sheer wishing and watching and calculating get the ship along faster or more directly to her goal. We now began a run that was fast enough to satisfy even my great impatience, for *Varua* was soon reeling off the fastest speeds she had ever made.

All that afternoon as the wind increased to near-gale

THE GREAT SOUTHERN SEA

force we tore on, heaving and lurching our way at ten knots and better through the long cross-seas, holding on to sail with a sort of lightheaded recklessness induced by the fair gale we had so wanted. It had been too long since we had sailed fast and free. Now for a few hours we tasted the speed inherent in *Varua* as she steered like an angel through the double-running seas, responding to the slightest movement of the wheel. I knew No. 2 and No. 3 staysails were likely to blow out any minute, but contrary to all indications they held and we ran on hour after hour. Then the wind began to shift, with increasing squalls and fine driving rain and drastically falling barometer, moving infallibly toward north, then east of north—and we still held on to our sails.

The great winds which should have been our allies had been our opponents for too long. Now for just twelve hours we had tasted our longed-for fair wind and had driven free. We were reluctant to give up our exhilarating speed and we hung on and drove the ship as she had never been driven before, ignoring the gyrations of the barograph, whose track for the last twenty-four hours looked like a roller coaster. After a weird momentary clearing at sunset that turned our sienna-colored sails into the deep red of Vatican velvet, black seething cloud masses blotted out the sky. As darkness closed down the gale increased, and the albatross were all around us in great numbers, soaring contentedly, at one with their real element.

The night was black and threatening. Gradually, as the wind shifted, we sheeted close, and the ship instead of being free was again strapped down, fighting to hold as near to course as possible, jarring as new seas from east of north began to rear and crash over the tops of the northwest seas. What had been a glorious wild ride became something of a desperate night ride—but no one except myself was in the least concerned. All that mattered was our progress.

For a few fleeting moments we glimpsed the growing moon just before it set; the barometer began to climb at a feverish rate. From time to time the beam from my big flashlight revealed the two upper staysails still holding together miraculously, but we had long since passed the margin of safety and to touch them then would have been to lose them. We were gambling that the wind had reached its peak, and carried on thinking only of the miles we were making, avoiding the thoughts that tried to crowd in as we hove through the blackness with the moan of wind in rigging and the strange steam-boiler noise along the hull, relying on a vastness of ocean and Tahitian eyes that see through darkness mine cannot penetrate.

We drove on. There was a throbbing shudder now and then when a crest passed under us; a sharp jar throughout the ship when one broke squarely against the hull. Along the lee waterline in the beam of the flashlight the foam rolled like smoke, hugging the ship for a brief moment until whipped away by a wind eddy. When I turned the light aloft I saw everything holding but I knew we had carried on too long. I knew that ships had been driven under, but *Varua* was too sure-footed for that.

We had never carried on like this before, and I was uncertain about whether we could even get the squaresails in without losing them. I was seriously worried about the topsail now, but only Tino and I working together stood a chance of getting the big sail in without the wind taking charge, and I dared not leave the wheel to go aloft because Zizi had never before had the helm under conditions like these. I did not want to lose the topsail but there was nothing we could do then. I worried through the dark hours,

THE GREAT SOUTHERN SEA

until finally in the dim dawn light, when I felt I could trust the wheel to Zizi to hold us dead before the wind, Tino and I went up and got it in—safely. Afterward I lingered up there while an albatross soared close by the yard, so close I could almost reach out and touch him in midair. We raced on, still almost on course—the foresail board-hard as it lifted the ship along; under me the narrow hull racing, the foam trail astern reaching just to the next crest before it was swallowed up.

Toward noon the wind let up somewhat and the sun glowed through the overcast for a few minutes just at its zenith—again just long enough for a sight. Later, two more sights gave me a good fix. I found we had done 233 miles noon to noon—the all-time record of my years of sailing.

With the northwest wind we had been able to edge out of the area in which icebergs might be encountered. As the wind drew east of north, however, we were gradually forced south of our course. By noon of February 3, after our record run, we were again within the danger area in 110° West Longitude. Another day would see us out of the area once and for all, for from here the curve swept deeply south to clear the Horn itself.

We had seen no signs of ice whatsoever and I began to breathe more easily as the day wore on. The sky cleared and the sea went down as the wind steadied to a moderate northeasterly breeze that seemed to bring some warmth with it. Visibility was better than it had been for a long time, so leaving Piho at the wheel, looking ridiculous in her man-size oilskins and boots, I went below and slept easily.

I awoke with the feeling that something was wrong. It was late afternoon. Glancing at the barograph on the way through the chartroom I noticed that it was moving up, leaving a peculiar jerky line. The sun was shining and Piho was dreamily steering to a light warm breeze as *Varua* forged slowly ahead. It seemed safe to hoist No. 3, which had been taken off for a squall earlier in the day. I ran the ship downwind to do so and in the five minutes before I had her back on course the beautiful sunny afternoon ended abruptly and bewilderingly. The sky and sea were suddenly veiled by what seemed at first to be a rain curtain moving in from all sides. I remember thinking how strange it was there were no birds, no albatross. Suddenly it dawned on me that this was fog—the first I had seen for many years. Visibility was down to perhaps a hundred yards or less. I took over again, tensely alert at the wheel as we forged slowly ahead through the gray emptiness. The wind died and we lay there in the waning day in an uncanny quiet, the calm sea adding to the eerie feeling that hung over us.

Out of the quiet came the sudden unnerving gasp of a whale blowing so close alongside that the mist from the spout drifted across my face before it had time to settle. I had been reading an account of a New Bedford whaler sunk by a whale, and of others lost in this region through collision with ice, and was thoroughly on edge.

The whale had no sooner gone his way than a new breeze came hesitatingly in from the south, carrying with it a biting chill that made me shiver under all my clothes. And was it my imagination or was there something strange in the air that my nostrils strained to catch? Did ice smell? When I had finished setting up the main-boom guy to the new wind and got back to the wheel, the fog was gone—as suddenly and as uncannily as it had come.

I did not see the ice at first. I was steering east and the horizon ahead was now clear and level. It was only when I looked south, then looked again more intently, that I saw it

THE GREAT SOUTHERN SEA

—low on the horizon, reflecting the flat rays of the late sun. Actually there were two masses visible, separated by a little distance, possibly two hummocks of ice on a single floe hidden beneath the horizon, or two small bergs. They lay there motionless, looking unreal, infinitely ominous.

A moment later the vagrant southerly breeze was gone, as was the biting chill in the air, and by the time I had slowly swept my binoculars around the circle of the horizon and made sure there were no other breaks in its continuity, a new breeze came in from the east and with it the fog again materialized from nowhere.

Throughout my watch, and on through Zizi's three hours from nine o'clock to twelve, I steered due north through the gray void, our masthead light glowing fuzzily in the shimmering damp vapor that lay over the sea. Just before it was time to call Tino at midnight the freshening wind shifted to north and miraculously the fog was gone, the stars shone, and the southern sea was clear in all directions.

At noon the next day we were at last well outside of the region where ice could be encountered. For ten days the little red circles with which I marked our noon positions on the chart had stepped erratically through the danger area. Had anyone suggested before leaving Tahiti that we would reach 50° S., I would have scoffed at the thought. For years I had been seduced by the literature and romance of the sailing-ship era, and in particular by the thought of experiencing in my own ship the adventure of running down our easting in the Roaring Forties. But my very familiarity with the subject would be enough to destroy any desire to get far enough south to be in the iceberg region. I knew too well the many ships lost to ice down there, among them, in 1928, the magnificent five-masted Danish barque *Kobenhavn* and its seventy cadets.

There is a fearsome meaning in the word ice for sailors. You can fight gales and seas but not ice. Our maneuverability gave us a great advantage over the big sailing ships that made twice our speed and took a half-mile and more to turn in. I felt that we would see ice in time, even at night. The masthead lookout just before dusk gave us reassurance for about an hour. Zizi and Tino took the two dark watches from 9 P.M. to 3 A.M., since Tahitian eyes can see much farther at night than mine. Daybreak came soon after 3 A.M. And so, once having been forced down there by the improbable succession of easterly gales, I was willing to take the chance and continue.

Curiously enough I had never even contemplated the possibility of ice plus fog, any more than I had dreamed of being down there in the first place. Fog made the danger much more acute, for as the sailing directions say:

In a dense fog an iceberg cannot be seen more than 100 yards ahead of the ship . . . a lookout will probably catch the first evidence of a berg by the breaking of the sea at its base or by growlers and fragments of ice from it.

In thick fog the echo from the foghorn is perhaps the only thing that might give warning in time. Most important of all is plain chance—in our case the chance that had us where we were rather than a few miles farther south. In any case we were now clear of the area and at last could breathe freely again.

4. THE ULTIMATE STORM

Ahead of us still lay a thousand miles of Roaring Forties, part of it with 10 per cent of gales or more. But we were now on the chart of the easternmost part of the South Pacific. Our destination, Valdivia, was over on the far edge, a much more explicit goal than an abstract compass course. The albatross, which had vanished during the fog, were back, among them a new variety that was black on top and had a black design under the shoulder. I looked forward to the simple problem of the Roaring Forties, uncomplicated by ice, as something of a rest cure. Such is the innocence and perennial optimism of the sailor.

At dark the wind whipped out of the northeast in a heavy squall. The barometer was falling fast. Still obsessed with carrying on to the limit to regain some of our lost time, I held on to the mainsail and nursed the ship until midnight, when the squall had not abated and it was apparent that this was another gale, again from the theoretically nonexistent northeast quadrant. In the glow of the masthead light we got the big sail down safely and secured it with extra lashings. No. 3 had long since been taken off. Now No. 2 was sent down to the saloon for repairs to the tack, which had started to open up again. Really bad weather was always the sign for us to make repairs to our two "expendables."

We carried on into the early morning hours under fore and main staysails, making fair time, thinking it was just another northeast gale, not knowing it was to be the culminating storm experience of my life. Anything I had previously seen was child's play compared with what was in store for us during the next forty-eight hours.

We were lying to under our fore staysail and lower main staysail, both of which were built for riding out gales. We lay on the port tack heading five or six points off the wind, forging slowly ahead and making visible leeway. Sometime around 3:30 A.M., when there was enough light for me to see the size and weight of the seas, I put out the oil bags. The effect of the slick on the breaking crests was at once apparent, but even under the two small storm staysails we were sailing too fast, leaving the oil astern. This was temporarily corrected by hauling the fore staysail somewhat to windward, increasing the leeway but stopping the forward motion. The seas were as big as any I had ever seen, perhaps thirty to thirty-five feet, and breaking heavily. We rode beautifully, taking hardly any water on deck.

All went well until sometime after daybreak when the seas reached such height and steepness that our sails were blanketed when in the trough and subjected to a terrific blast on the crest. When the wind began to tear off whole chunks of sea from the crests and hurl them across our deck into the sails I took them off.

We put extra lashings around all the sails. Everything else was already snug and secure. Boats and rope cage had all the lashings that could be passed through the ringbolts. Storm covers were on all hatches. There is never loose gear on deck.

Finding her natural drift, with wheel lashed amidships, *Varua* fell off several points and drifted slowly downwind with the seas on her quarter, driven and steadied by the wind on her bare masts and yards. In spite of the increasing wind and sea she was easier and drier than she had been before, and the oil slick was obviously more effective.

The barometer had fallen half an inch in a few hours. The speed with which wind and sea built up was amazing. The familiar moan of the gale in the rigging increased to a new high-pitched wail. But *Varua* was taking care of herself well, so I worked off my nervous energy doing two jobs I had been putting off: cleaning the engine-room bilge suction, and taking up a section of floor to retrieve a lost wrench.

Gradually during the day the gale shifted from northeast to north, but slowly enough so that the seas shifted with it. The ship continued to handle herself nicely, coming up gradually as the wind shifted, keeping it on her quarter. The oil seemed to reduce the power of the breaking crests so that no solid water came aboard. The barometer had stopped its downward rush at 29.50 and was leveling off. The sea was the most impressive I had ever experienced but the whole thing had developed so fast I was convinced it would blow itself out in a matter of hours.

I was wrong. As night fell both wind and sea were worse and I began to feel uneasy. The barometer now remained steady. Oil bags were renewed just before dark, with foul-smelling but effective fish oil that had been aboard ever since 1945 when we left Gloucester. We also had two small drums of heavy coconut oil from Tahiti to experiment with, but it had solidified from the cold and was useless.

Nothing was said, but all of us gathered that evening in the saloon. The ship underwent increasingly violent gyrations, and had that cello-like tremble throughout that goes with real gale winds. Through the cabin windows—buried deep one moment, carving great arcs across the sky the next—we caught a glimpse now and then of the growing moon, momentarily visible between flying clouds. I could not help thinking, as I felt the seas crash outside, of the fragile fabric that made up this small ship—man and his little toy—pitted against what was outside. What was more vulnerable, what more dependent upon each individual part? I turned on the radio to drown out the noise of the storm and surprisingly it functioned perfectly. We listened to South American music. We made jokes about South American weather, and laughed too loudly at our jokes.

At 9 P.M. I wrote in the log that "the storm is at its worst." Again I was wrong. From then on things got worse instead of better. The ship jarred more heavily from breaking crests, in spite of the oil. The shriek of wind and the vibration of the whole structure increased—but my confidence that the ship could take care of herself was still unshaken.

At 11 P.M. I told the others to try to get some rest, and lay down for a fitful nap myself, only to be awakened a half hour later by a jarring crash as if we had been struck by a pile driver. It was obvious that *Varua* was in trouble now and needed help. Putting on oilskins I went to the wheel.

As soon as my eyes had become adjusted to the blackness of the night I could see what was happening. The mechanical action of the rolling seas, now towering incredibly steep and high, had overcome her natural downwind drift. Nearing the top of a sea, the wind blast would heel her over, get a grip on her forward top hamper, and start to drive her downwind as before. Then the crest would strike her on the quarter, counteracting the wind. Finally, falling down the steep back side of the sea, cut off from the wind, she would slide broadside to. This was final, dangerous proof of what

I had always feared: that letting a ship take her natural drift would not work when conditions produced a disproportionately high, steep sea.

To satisfy my curiosity once and for all I left her this way a little longer to find out if it was true that "a good ship left alone will always take care of herself." The seas were so huge and concave at this point that the whole upper third seemed to collapse and roar vertically down on us. Our oil had little or no effect now, as the surface water was all being blown to leeward. After feeling the shock of two or three of the more moderate seas crashing down on us I felt I had carried my scientific investigation far enough. I unlashed the wheel and with no effort at all ran her off downwind before one of the real monsters chanced to break on us. I am convinced that, although her hull structure might have withstood the battering, boats and everything else on deck would have been swept away, and most likely masts as well.

Realizing at last that this was building toward the ultimate conditions I had never yet encountered, I ran *Varua* off dead before it. In choosing to run as a final emergency tactic I was going against all the books. I thanked my stars we did not have a sea anchor out, for nothing in the world outside of being moored to an island would have held her head into the wind and seas that were now running.

The seas were white phosphorescent avalanches that I felt towering over my head astern but did not see until they burst down on us and swept by on either side. Although under bare poles, *Varua* picked up speed and began running six or seven knots, dangerously, but steering beautifully. We at once put out drags and slowed her down to about three knots, which still left her with good rudder control. It took a seventy-five-fathom, two-inch-diameter

Manila line which we dragged in a big bight, plus four seventy-five-foot mooring lines of the same size, each dragging its big eye splice, plus about a hundred fathoms of assorted lines of smaller size.

Moving slowly ahead as we now were we could lay an oil slick right along our path and astern. Sometimes, to my astonishment, the wind picked up so much surface water that it even carried some of our oil ahead of us. Conditions being extreme we kept two oil bags on each side, lashed outboard to the channels so that they could not be thrown by the seas, and pumped oil steadily through a toilet down below. It is difficult to say how much good it did, but it seemed to me that the seas broke less frequently on us than at a little distance to either side, and less heavily.

It was 11:30 P.M. when I took the wheel and began to run. It was noon the following day before a tendency to abate made it safe to turn the ship over to Tino. During those twelve and a half hours we fought a battle so crucial that had any one of the great breaking seas caught us off balance we would have been swept. At the very least this would have meant the loss of boats.

Shifting imperceptibly from north to northwest, the storm reached a peak at around 2 A.M. It is banal to use the term "hurricane" as it is so misused, particularly in the accounts of sailing craft. But I have experienced several recorded hurricanes in my life, both on land and at sea, and this was worse than any of them. Before the wind had reached its peak there had been a whole new set of shrieks and howls in the rigging and fittings. I now learned something entirely new: that when the wind exceeds a certain point most of these noises stop, and this was more ominous than ever.

From time to time I began to hear what I thought was thunder—a hollow booming that reverberated through the night—not realizing at first that it was the sound of great seas breaking. But these were seas greater by far than any I had ever before seen.

With all our drags astern, and bare poles, we sailed our steady three or four knots through the water—except when the crests passed under us and we rode them at breathtaking speed. When I spoke of the culminating experience of a life of voyaging, this is what I had in mind. When a fifty-ton, seventy-foot vessel surfboards shudderingly down the face of a great sea on its breaking crest, you have experienced something.

At these times she was going downhill at such a steep angle that when she reached the bottom she would bury her bowsprit before rising: an excellent object lesson, for if she had been carrying any sail, or even running under bare poles without drags, she would probably have gone right on down.

This was now a fight to save the ship—the final great test which *Varua* had been built to survive. I remembered the design days, bent over the drafting table with Starling Burgess.

"Her rudder must be above all worry," I had said, and that had been easy—a simple matter of engineering.

And when all the other details had been surmounted there remained the last, the most important of all.

"She must be able to run before it with safety in any weather."

It was against prevailing opinion to choose as a last resort to run with great breaking seas, but I knew instinctively that there would come a point when you could no longer hold her into it, either by drags, sea anchors, riding sails, or any other means. When that point was reached it would probably be too late to turn and run.

I remembered our anxious trips to Stevens Institute with the hull model for tank testing. Special apparatus had been devised to simulate following seas. At first her stern had been more conventional; but she had a tendency to pull the following seas over on top of her and even to broach to. Little by little the stern was changed and the rest of the underwater lines accordingly, until one day we had a model that did not disturb the form of the following sea, that did not trip, that ran true before it at all speeds. We called it her "double chin" stern.

Varua had always performed beautifully, but she had never fought for her life before. Starling Burgess is dead now, so he will never know. I like to think that his spirit was there watching, for *Varua* met her test like the thoroughbred she is, running true and clean. Never once that night or the following morning did she make a false move, or fail to lift when she should, or fail to respond to every move of the wheel.

That night was the only time I have felt acute danger of being bodily injured by a sea. There was a double Manila line around my waist, made fast to the bitts beside me, so I could hardly have been washed overboard. But if I were beaten unconscious by a breaking sea and the ship broached to out of control it would amount to the same thing. The danger in these seas lay in the fact that they were unnaturally short compared to their towering, almost perpendicular height. They had built up so incredibly fast against the old easterly sea that they had had no time to lengthen out.

There was fear in the air that night as the great blazing hollow crests hung over my head blotting out half the sky. My body tried to shrink down into the steering well for shelter. My hands spun the wheel instinctively to maintain control and keep the keel exactly in line with the sea as we made the trembling rush on the crest.

From time to time the others passed up mugs of hot soup through the six-inch compass hole in the after side of the charthouse. Someone would shout through the hole the latest barometer reading, as I tried to gulp the soup between seas before the wind siphoned it away into the air. The work at the wheel was physically and nervously exhausting, not only from the strenuous exertion but from the sheer weight of wind which seemed of only slightly less substance than the sea itself. The dark low-ceilinged sky seemed to press upon me. There was a feeling of continuity about the gale, of timelessness. In a sort of coma I steered automatically down the face of the great breaking seas. Everything combined to produce weariness—except my growing confidence in *Varua*.

Sometime around three o'clock in the morning, before daybreak, a sea larger than any of the others broke just as our stern started to lift to it. Tino and Zizi had taken turns pumping oil out through the forward toilet. Possibly there was a lull in the slick just then, as the men changed shifts. More probably this sea was just so big that nothing could stop or soften it. I had felt it building up in the ominous calm after two or three other great seas had lifted us, and began to tense myself some time before it struck. We had several times been swept by broken water as crests carried us along, or by a cross-sea that came in from the wrong direction, but not by one of the main seas.

This time we were under one of the boomers. As *Varua* lifted on the body of the wave the breaking crest hung high overhead and as it broke I braced myself as low as I could get in the well, holding the wheel in a vicelike grip. It crashed on me with a tremendous blow, burying the entire after part of the ship under solid water but pouring off on either side by the time it got past the charthouse. I remember hoping just as it hit me on the back that no big fish was lurking in the crest.

Even under the tremendous power exerted by this sea *Varua* continued to respond to the helm and held straight on her course dead before it. A moment later came the shouted report through the slot in the compass hole that everything was all right below. Water had spurted through hatches that had always been tight, but that was all.

I had felt that my physical endurance might fail. The immersion in ice water brought me out of my fatigue with a vengeance. And when I saw how the ship handled herself with her whole after part immersed under the weight of a great sea I felt a spiritual lift that released in me the extra forces that we call up to carry us through times of great crisis. I was probably still as cold and bone weary as it is possible to get, but the relief from the ultimate crisis made things seem almost agreeable.

Again and again that night, I asked myself why I was there—and had no better answer than that perhaps this was the very thing that had drawn me into this voyage: an unexpressed urge to experience a real Cape Horn gale. We were not off Cape Horn, but we were close enough for this to be the real thing. And along with the fear that was in the air that night was the exultation that came with the knowledge that the ship would always respond, and that wind of this force could not go on forever, and that I could go on and on, instinctively meeting each sea as it came until the storm was over . . . and perhaps to know this was the reason I was there.

By daybreak the glass was rising slowly and by 10 A.M. I would have let Tino take her. He came and crouched by

THE ULTIMATE STORM

me, on the other side of the wheel, but was too appalled by the size of the seas to take the responsibility. They were still destructive, the wind in the squalls still screamed, but things were appreciably better. Not until noon would he take her alone. By this time the destructive force was obviously slackening although there was still plenty of danger.

The gale had started in the northeast. It had piled up the worst seas from northwest at the height of its fury. Now it had shifted to west. One had to decide which seas were the worst and meet them, allowing the lesser ones to hit us off balance. And as the wind eased, some of the seas got out of control, becoming what I call "crazy seas," which tower up into a huge pyramid and break quite unpredictably. You could not meet one of these crazy seas as you did the more conventional ones—you just hoped you weren't there.

It was 5 P.M. when we started to get the drags in, a simple matter of heaving them in one at a time. At 6 P.M. we tried the main staysail on her to feel out the seas under way, leaving two or three drag lines still out and keeping on with the oil. A little later we added the fore staysail and were able to sail our course with the seas on our quarter, seas that were now lengthening out and losing their punch. We hauled in the last of the drags and went on our way, undamaged, but smelling to high heaven of fish oil, sailing in seas that were still greater than any I had previously experienced, but that now, by comparison, seemed perfectly safe. The wind was around to southwest now, and as we resumed our regular watches we were able to steer our course for Patagonia.

Released from captivity just before dark, when the crests were no longer dangerous, eleven-year-old Piho scrambled out at once into the steering well demanding permission to bathe in the rain. Her brown body was covered by only a scrap of red *pareu* around her middle. I don't suppose it would have hurt her, but the thought of it made me shudder in my woolens, boots, and two suits of oilskins. I sent her below to bathe where it was somewhat warmer, but a little later as I was going through my own ritual preliminary to turning in I wondered if perhaps a bath in the rain, no matter how cold, was to Piho what my shave was to me. For tense and tired as I was, I let down slowly, bathing, shaving, eating leisurely with Ah You at the gimbal table—savoring to the full the exquisite satisfaction of peace after storm before going contentedly to my berth.

The morning after the storm Tino let me sleep right through my dawn watch. There was a wonderful unspoken understanding between Tino and myself. He was supposed to wake me at 3 A.M. every morning for my watch, although he never did. Normally I would wake up anyway, but when I was behind in sleep I would get an extra half hour or so before my built-in alarm system began to function. Later, when I had the wheel during the day, I would repay him by letting him oversleep his nap. This particular morning I slept right on until the smell of breakfast filtered vaguely through to my subconscious. The whole day was vague, as a matter of fact. It was nothing very much as days went, with an unpleasant squally wind; but it was a fair wind at last, from southwest, and we were all under that strange lightheaded intoxication that comes after great fatigue—content with the realization that we and the ship had surpassed ourselves in what was probably the greatest test of our lives. We had between us that extra something that creates an unspoken bond between people who have come through a great ordeal together.

During the hours of trial I had thought of nothing but

THE ULTIMATE STORM

security, comfort—even of quitting the sea forever and using *Varua* as a houseboat. Now, after a good night's sleep, the dual nature of the seafarer asserted itself, and I realized that probably never, in any other life, would I feel as fit as I did now.

By midday we must have been sailing as fast as we ever did. With the wind in the southwest, on our quarter, all our sails pulled to the greatest advantage. That is, all except No. 3, which was down in the saloon being reinforced and which could not have been carried anyway, for the wind must have been near gale force although we were still too numb from the great storm to feel it.

Looking back, I realize that we were carrying practically full sail under conditions that would have had us shortened way down before the storm. Already we referred to it as *the* storm, and always would. Most of the time we had been driving as usual in the direction of the Horn. It was a relief to be racing at top speed toward Valdivia for a change, under conditions that were at last ideal for our brigantine rig with its tremendous lifting power.

Night came and we were still flying. The following seas carried us with them but they were longer now and did not feel dangerous. They were still the seas from our storm, but spread out more. On my first night watch I was conscious enough to realize vaguely that something magnificent was occurring—Sibelius's *Night Ride* kept running round and round in my head—but I was still in a semicomatose state and only half noticed how fast the phosphorescence was flying past the racing hull. We must have been sailing even faster than during the night of February 2, when we made our record run of 233 miles, for when noon came the next day, February 8, we had run 240 miles and this will, without doubt, remain the greatest day's run of my life.

It is ironic that during the only twenty-four-hour period of the voyage in which we had the weather of the fairy stories, I was still in such a state of numbness from the experience we had been through that it hardly registered. Of the first twelve hours I remember very little except a lot of violent motion which interfered with our effort to scrub the fish oil smell from the ship down below. And at night there was *Night Ride*.

It was only on the following morning when I took the wheel from Tino and waited for the dawn that it really began to register. When it was light enough to see I realized that here at last was the southern ocean of literature: "The Brave West Winds roaring fresh behind us and the mile long seas breaking high . . ." But even so I was not prepared for the 240 miles when I laid down our noon position, so little so that I took additional sights, and rechecked the previous day's figures as well, to be sure it was true.

These two great runs that *Varua* made are probably not records compared with the big ocean-racing yachts with their mountain of sail nursed by large crews, but considering how under-sparred and under-canvased *Varua* is, to allow me to sail her with two men, I think it is going some. And in both cases we were sailing east, or nearly so, and the period from noon to noon was sixteen minutes less than twenty-four hours due to the time we gained on the sun. These two days, plus two more on which we did respectively 202 and 170 miles, were the only days on the entire voyage when we were able to run free on our course. It is interesting to speculate that had it been possible to maintain the 211-mile average of these four days with really fair winds, we might have sailed from Rapa to Corral over the 3,800-mile route originally planned in just eighteen days.

THE ULTIMATE STORM

Filled with elation at the fantastic day's run we had made, we even forgot to resent the squalls and fine cold driving rain that plagued us all the following night.

After this I realized we had nothing to fear from the southern ocean any more. We were well clear of the ice limits. Ahead lay several five-degree squares with 10 per cent and 12 per cent gales—but no gale could ever frighten us after our storm. We were well into our last thousand miles, putting our destination within grasp. One can get one's mind around a few hundred miles. In the thousands it is better not to think, but to live from day to day. Now there was the growing mystery and excitement of approaching landfall. The little necklace of tiny circles on the chart representing noon positions had crept across the empty spaces, sometimes going in the right direction, sometimes not, until now the thin chain had almost reached Chile. Two or three more would complete the circuit.

The next day was beautiful and we made a fine run. The wind was back in the northwest. For the second time since we entered southern latitudes, the sky was clear. At noon the thermometer was up to 61° F. and by midafternoon to 65° F. I kept repeating in the log "beautiful day," ignoring the big noon halo around the sun, for I was through worrying about signs. After a good sleep I got out the books on the Cape Horners again. We felt like Cape Horners now. It had been uncanny how we had been constantly forced in the direction of the Horn. Tino had started referring to it as our Cape Horn voyage, and soon the others followed suit. If it had not been for Ah You's condition and the nearness of the approaching event I think we might have taken the line of least resistance and sailed on around.

TO THE GREAT SOUTHERN SEA

Relaxing in the sun on the transom at the foot of the companionway, I reread the saga of the last of the great Cape Horners that had passed this way in the twilight of the great days of sail, and especially of the Finnish fleet of Gustaf Erickson. These ships were the culmination of the knowledge man had stored up over the ages in building and rigging great ocean sailers. Like *Varua* they had met their great test in these waters. The lucky ones made a fast passage to the Horn and home. The others fell by the wayside dismasted, perhaps driven under, or kept a rendezvous at night with ice and oblivion like the *Kobenhavn*. Perhaps the lucky ones were those that never came home, for they were spared the ignominy of ending their days as coal hulks, or the ultimate disgrace of the breakup yards.

Our trail had followed the route of these last great windjammers. The names ran clearly through my memory: the *Herzogin Cecilie, Grace Harwar, Lawhill, Olivebank, Penang,* and all the others. I could almost imagine the ghosts of the great ships booming along before their westerly gales. Our gales had all been easterly; perhaps the westerlies had died with the windjammers.

Thinking of the crews who sailed them down these latitudes—cold and wet for weeks—I realized that they would have considered our mild hardships a life of luxury, eased as they were by hot meals, dry clothes, good quarters, and a warm galley to retreat to.

As I read I glanced up through the companionway at little Piho at the wheel, steering the ship through green seas that still ran high, her pigtails escaped from under her oversize yellow southwester hat. I could almost hear the vanished crews turning over in their graves to cry out in horror at this final insult of an eleven-year-old Tahitian girl alone on deck steering a sailing ship through the Roaring Forties.

THE ULTIMATE STORM

That night we had one more wild ride, as usual to the accompaniment of the fine steady rain that prevails in these parts. Vaguely defined squalls built up the wind, now in the northwest, to the danger point for the upper staysails. No. 3 was furled at daybreak to preserve it, while I tried to carry No. 2 on through, expecting the wind to ease up with the sun. But the clew let go at 4:30 A.M., and this perennially expendable sail was again brought down to the saloon for repairs. Both Tino and Zizi had shaved at 4 A.M. while waiting around for orders as I debated taking off the topsail. By 5 A.M. they were sewing on No. 2. I was struck by the fact that our unnatural hours had become so habitual that nobody thought anything of them.

There was the usual slack period shortly after sunrise. No. 2 was repaired by then, so Tino went aloft and bent it again. Before the wind came back full force it was set and drawing once more. Our run could not equal the other two record days, but it was good for 202 miles noon to noon, after which the wind shifted suddenly back to southwest after rather startling barometer gyrations, and it fell calm and that was the end of our "westerlies" passage.

Even Ah You recovered now, with the calm easy motion and the thought of approaching landfall. The weeks of dismal sickness were gone and the future was bright again. She put on a gaily colored *pareu*, combed her long hair, and with shining eyes got out the guitar and sang Paumotu songs.

There were two days of light shifting breezes and calms and crazy seas and the voyage was almost done. *Varua* was a beehive of activity, the two girls singing down below as they waxed and polished and prepared the ship for landfall. Zizi, inspired by their example, fell to and cleaned the galley as it had never been cleaned before. Work done, Tino and Zizi would sit together at the wheel talking endlessly, with the enthusiasm of Tahitians, who are never bored. They had been nearly five thousand miles together now and were still not talked out. To our great joy we caught our first fish since leaving Tahiti, an enormous tuna. We ate fish for breakfast, lunch, and supper—raw, boiled, baked, fried.

The albatross were leaving us now. Only one was left and he seemed to be as reluctant to leave us as we were to see him go. Those great birds are in truth the "Friend of the Cape Horner." The last I saw of him he was floating disconsolately and disheveled on the sea—perhaps waiting for wind to help him take off.

On February 13, when we were five thousand miles out and had only three hundred to go to Port Corral, our old enemy the northeaster came back at us for a last effort. To the end it would have been easier to go around the Horn. It was a brisk rainy twenty-four-hour gale. We knew all its tricks, except the weird sea it produced blowing against a huge southwest swell, but it drove us south again to make our landfall far down on the rugged islands off the Patagonian coast. When this last brief gale blew itself out there was no wind left, and we were becalmed only a day's sail from land. The shore birds were all around us. We were avid to see the coast and impatiently started the engine and went on to make landfall under power over an undulating sea that was as smooth as patent leather.

5. LANDFALL

At sunset there had been a tentative breeze from the west, but it was soon killed by heavy black rain squalls. As night fell we were again surrounded by albatross of several kinds, most of them resting on the uneasily heaving sea.

At 9 P.M. Zizi came to take the wheel. I went down to service the engine before turning in for my watch below. An hour later I was still idling in the engine room, half wanting to stop the engine to drag out the last few miles. Eventually I turned in, too embarrassed to communicate my thoughts to the others. The engine was still running.

"By sunrise we will see the land," I had told them. But as I lay in my berth thinking of the old navigators who had passed this way, I felt that we had an almost unfair advantage. They would not have been able to make such a statement. Their longitude might be hundreds of miles out, while we had been able to check our chronometer throughout the voyage by radio time signals from Station WVV in Washington and knew our longtitude to within a half-dozen miles. The advantage this gave us is easy to imagine for we approached one of the most desolate and hazardous coasts in the world.

The movement of the ship was unfamiliar without the pressure of wind in sails but the slow rhythmic pulse of the diesel put me to sleep almost at once.

In the morning the land was there, seen intermittently through rain squalls: the desolate storm-lashed archipelago off the Patagonian coast. Beyond, unseen in the murk, lay the mainland. Later there was bright sun for a while, which made it possible to check our position accurately. We were farther south than expected, having allowed during the night for a considerable northerly current which had not materialized. With the sun came whales, a tuna on our line, and a little warmth. *Varua*'s crew was wreathed in broad smiles. We could have been cruising in far milder, safer latitudes.

With land in sight I raced excitedly through the Sailing Directions trying to find a way to get into the Patagonian channels with reasonable safety. Since we had been unable to get charts for the coast of Chile before leaving Tahiti, we had planned to stop at Valdivia first to get them. Valdivia is an important town ten miles up a navigable river. After a long hard sea voyage a wide river winding peacefully through green foothills would be close to heaven.

Valdivia's port of entry, Port Corral, was simplicity itself to get into, with deep-water approach, perfect shelter, and pilots. In Valdivia we could rest, buy charts, and get local information for the Patagonian channels.

We were so far behind schedule that I had almost given up hope of exploring the archipelago with *Varua*. The brief Patagonian summer was almost over. By the time we made Valdivia, did what was necessary, and worked south again, it would be too late. But here we were, three hundred miles south of Valdivia due to northeast gales, and there seemed to be a spell of unprecedented calm weather. Perhaps we could salvage something in spite of the lateness of the season.

It was a challenge not to be ignored. The question was how to get in without charts.

LANDFALL

The key to the problem, if any, was to be found in the volume of Sailing Directions that lay open before me on the chart table—Hydrographic Office No. 173, that covers, among other things, the six hundred miles from Corcovado Gulf to Magellan Straits, and the even more remote reaches from Cape Pilar to the Horn itself.

Held back by inner caution and responsibilities, but insidiously attracted by the region in spite of everything, I read again the already well-thumbed pages concerning the intricate maze of islands, channels, and fiords that made up the Patagonian archipelago. There were items concerning fir-fringed glacier-fed fiords, virgin forests, volcanoes, even hot springs. There was a hidden sound where trapped icebergs floated majestically in smooth water the year round. Eternally snow-capped mountains towered over the channels. There was even one place where you could anchor in a secure cove with a thousand-foot waterfall roaring into the headwaters of the bay. I have always had a weakness for waterfalls, and would have paid dearly to have anchored *Varua* in that cove. Moreover, the usually restrained Sailing Directions lost all reticence when it came to the Patagonian archipelago, enumerating and repeating difficulties so overwhelming that the challenge became hard to resist:

Thick tempestuous weather is the normal state.

Almost perpetual rain, thick weather, strong gales; heavy williwaws which must be felt to be believed.

Breaks of fine weather sometimes but rare and short.

Average rainfall 11 hours out of 24.

Hailstorms and snow flurries even in summer.

Waterspouts . . . which can swamp an open boat in a few minutes.

Chasm-like channels where wind and current funnel through with such force that full-powered steamers must wait the slack.

Vessels carrying sail often capsized.

I thought I saw a way to get in to the archipelago. Beyond Guafo Island (eighty days per year with gales) which we could now make out clearly, lay the wide *boca* leading to Corcovado Gulf. There were "strong eddies and tide rips" in the *boca,* but the currents were only three to four knots—very modest for these parts. Just inside the strait, facing the fiords and snow-capped mountains of the Patagonian mainland, lay a small sheltered harbor, Port Melinca—"the only inhabited port between Corcovado Gulf and Magellan Strait." Kelp would show us the shoals as we approached the harbor.

Port Melinca was apparently a calm spot surrounded by gales, for it was said to have them only four days per year in spite of being only about forty miles from Guafo Island with its average of eighty days.

If we could get to Melinca we could find charts and local knowledge, explore the fiords, and work north inside the Chiloé archipelago to Puerto Montt. Here we could go outside again via the famous Chacao Channel and follow the coast up to Valdivia.

"Let's try it," I told Tino, and gave him the new course.

To bring us in we had the little frontispiece map of H.O. No. 173 and a sketch which I had made of courses and bearings. The book warned that "great care should be taken to unmistakably recognize Isla Guafo" in order to avoid entering the wrong strait. We came close enough to make out landmarks with the binoculars but then stayed well clear, for the island fully justified its ominous description. Several miles off we felt the trembling in the air as the mighty Pacific swells broke against the base of the cliffs.

The weather was still co-operating as we passed Guafo and entered the strait. The great gulf lay open ahead. To starboard stretched the maze of islands that sheltered Moraleda Channel from the sea. North of us we could see the Chiloé archipelago. Miraculously the strait was calm.

Gradually the haze lifted until suddenly we saw the glint of sun on snow peaks beyond the gulf. Visibility increased as we edged cautiously around Guaitecas Island looking for landmarks to lead us in. Soon the whole coastal range lay clear—a study in black and white that reminded me of a Rockwell Kent etching.

We were close in, only a few miles from shelter, when the tide turned. A sudden boiling millrace stopped us in our tracks. At the same time, fast black clouds swept in very low from the west and the world became almost dark. According to the directions, a period of warm and calm weather with unusual visibility followed without warning by a fast darkening sky comes just before bad weather, usually from the west. Corcovado Gulf is entirely open to the westward.

There was no choice. We turned tail and retreated to sea, running out between Guafo and the southern end of Chiloé Island. The tide rip, plus a brisk squall wind from the southwest, swept us the first few miles at breathtaking speed as we drove hard under sail and power to get an offing before night. We felt the power of the westerly swell as we took it on the bow for a change.

Early in the night things looked less threatening, only wind squalls and bursts of rain having developed. At midnight there was a fresh northeast breeze. We cut our flight to sea and worked north off the coast of Chiloé, watching the weather constantly. The grim desolate coast crept by, mile after mile, rugged hills rising blackly from the sea. Although the weather seemed all right, it was not a reassuring position.

There was still one more chance to get in. If we could make Ancud, just inside the north end of Chiloé Island, there would be pilots for Chacao Channel and Puerto Montt, the northern port for the Patagonian channels and an excellent harbor for both large and small vessels. The passage through Chacao Channel sounded like the experience of a lifetime, it being a deep-water slot fourteen miles long and only one mile wide connecting the gulfs of Coronados and Ancud, with currents up to nine knots and no slack water.

When dawn came and there was still nothing worse than occasional squalls we felt safer and worked in close to the land. Chiloé looked most inhospitable, with the sea beating at the foot of cliffs. The dense forests were broken now and then by slopes of cleared land. We wondered what sort of people could eke out an existence here.

As we approached the northern end of the island, I stood in the companionway with the Sailing Directions, translating aloud into French as I read for the benefit of Ah You and Piho, who were sharing the wheel between them. Tino and Zizi were up forward performing the sailor's favorite chore, passing the chain on deck and shackling it onto the anchor. As they worked, they shouted a ribald Tahitian ballad at the top of their lungs. I reread what the Sailing Directions had to say about the tides, which seemed to be all there was to worry about:

> The rise and fall of tide in the region of the Gulfs of Ancud and Corcovado is greater than any other part of Chile except the eastern entrance of Magellan Strait, reaching as high as 23 feet rise and fall.
>
> The waters have the appearance of a rapid river, with rips and whirls of great strength. With strong winds contrary to the tides, great agitation of the waters takes place, called *rayas*.

LANDFALL

The *raya* of Ancud was said to be dangerous even to large vessels, but the chance of our meeting it seemed slight. I had no way of calculating the time the tide rip would form in the strait approaching Ancud Bay but it was reasonable to assume that it would occur more or less simultaneously with that of Corcovado. That being the case it would be an hour later than the previous day, giving us ample time to get into Ancud beforehand.

As we rounded the northern point of Chiloé we could see several weatherbeaten farms checkering the forested slopes. *Varua* was sailing fast, heeling before a new northwest wind backed by threatening black cloud banks across the whole western horizon. The glass was again falling hard. Before me was a sketch chart I had made of the approaches to Ancud from bearings and descriptions in the Sailing Directions.

We skirted the outer kelp beds and steered into the Gulf of Coronados, feeling like Ulysses facing Charybdis. If we could just get within sight of Ancud the pilot would see our signal and come out. We progressed nicely for a mile or so until we encountered a noisy rush of white water with short steep breaking seas from all directions, exactly as in Corcovado Gulf the previous day. Two or three miles farther in was smooth water, across which a small steamer placidly moved toward Ancud Bay. We gained a little more while the tide gathered its forces. Then the *raya*, if it was the *raya*, threw us out bodily—sternwards—in spite of a strong quartering wind and full speed on the engine.

Patagonia certainly had her defenses up.

There were still three or four hours before nightfall, but the cloud banks that had whirled up in the west swept in from the sea and made it suddenly almost dark. I began to wonder if this was a daily routine, but wasted no time in making an offing.

At first it seemed reasonable to spend the night at sea and try again in the morning when the tide would presumably be flowing instead of ebbing. But when night fell, with more and more weight in the squalls and the barometer acting peculiarly, the only sensible thing seemed to be to make all possible speed toward Corral and Valdivia. We resolutely headed north, with about one hundred miles to go.

We were giving up what had been an almost miraculous chance to get *Varua* into the Patagonian archipelago. We had almost made it but it had not come off. I half acknowledged to myself what I had known all along: that the way to see the Patagonian channels was in a local vessel with local knowledge. But I was still unwilling to give up completely the hope that some day, somehow, we might get back down there—on *Varua.*

It was a tense last night, with the barometer giving phrenetic warning of something—possibly the long-expected westerly gale. If it would just hold off for another twelve hours—for we were following a lee shore to make port: the most critical phase of a voyage.

As we plodded heavily north the squalls increased in weight and we made spurts of nine or ten knots. Shortly after nightfall we heard a sound like an express train going over a long bridge, and all hands rushed to get the sails off faster than they had ever come off before. *Varua* heeled shudderingly under bare poles to a cold blast of wind and rain from the southeast—straight out of Coronados Gulf. It was one of those that "must be felt to be believed." *Varua* recovered her balance, gathered steerageway, and rushed off nakedly into the night without a scrap of canvas.

LANDFALL

The glass jumped up, and down, and up again. Then there was rain but no wind and the glass dropped way down, until there was a sudden new blast from northeast and again *Varua* heeled, gathered way, and rushed off dizzily into the night.

It was suddenly much colder, for these blasts came from snow-capped mountains. When this one blew itself out the rain curtain swept out to sea and revealed Point Galera lighthouse. We stared at the light, hypnotized.

There was a moon behind clouds. The shore loomed high and black through the night—jagged, cruel, eternal—unbroken, except for the cut at Panama, all the way to the Arctic Ocean.

At 2:30 A.M. we were abeam Galera light. The wind was again in the northwest. We were sailing briskly along as if nothing had happened. Two hours later we hove to five miles off Morro Gonzalo to wait for daylight, 4,740 miles and thirty-seven days out of Rapa. Morro Gonzalo is the landmark for the entrance to Port Corral, Valdivia . . . and heaven.

The wind had gone full west now. There was rain off and on. The barometer seemed to be taking a deep breath from its gyrations of the night.

Let it blow from the west now, I thought. Let the long-threatening gale burst on the coast. Hidden behind the sharp bend of the point looming blackly through the night —it is called Laurel Point in the book—was shelter from the sea. In an hour or so it would be light enough to enter. The voyage was all but done.

There were stars now, blotted out from time to time by low fast clouds from the west. I lay on my back on deck beside the lashed wheel. *Varua* nudged the seas gently as she waited; the two lower staysails were barely enough to give her steerageway for the surface wind was now light.

As I lay there, watching the racing clouds, I thought how different this voyage had been from any I had previously made. Some days the interminable cold, gales, and head winds had been almost too much. It would have been so easy to run north to warm friendly latitudes—to the trade winds, Mangareva, the atolls, and home to Tahiti.

At times I had considered turning back because of Ah You. I would ask her how bad it was.

"I will tell you if it gets too bad," she would say. "How far is it now to South America?"

Although temptation was there I knew deep down that there was no turning back. One does not abandon one's goals as easily as that. And besides, I had promised Ah You her baby would be born in the Canal Zone.

There was also the question of solitude. There had been solitude before, on the other voyages, but never the out-of-this-world solitude of the southern ocean. For six weeks we had been where ships no longer pass, starkly aware of the complete interdependence of our little group of five souls—six according to Ah You's count—and *Varua*. As long as we did everything right we were all right; or should have been, for chance and fate are also to be reckoned with. It was reasonable to think of leaving one's bones in some warm tropical sea, to be stirred now and then perhaps by a tropical cyclone or brushed by the passing shadow of some gay young circumnavigator—but down in this dismal gray remoteness, chilled by the drifting Antarctic ice, was no place to die.

All deep-water sailors feel opposing emotions about the sea. Love and hate—even fear—all play their part. Never, before this voyage, had I felt the threat of the sea so acutely;

never had my love of the sea been so seriously threatened by the opposing emotions.

Another novelty of this voyage was that for the first time, once it was over, I questioned my strategy. I will never know whether the determined hunt for the westerlies, even to 50° S., was the right move. Perhaps we would have found fairer winds if we had stayed up near 40°. But we would have missed the experience of a lifetime.

There was no uncertainty about our storm. If I live to be a hundred it will still be *the* storm. Nor was there doubt about the effectiveness of *Varua*'s rig, its remarkable ease of handling being second only to the amazing lack of chafe, usually the bugbear of long ocean voyages. Once the flaw in the mainsail slide attachments was corrected there was no further trouble whatsoever.

As far as nervous strain goes the record is not so good. Although I was no doubt the only one who seemed to be bothered by it, the incessant whine of strong winds in rigging was definitely wearing. I had first read of this in connection with Antarctic expeditions and had first known it on Taiaro, my atoll in the Tuamotus. On this voyage I had felt it acutely, even more than the cold.

When I called chafe the bugbear of long ocean voyages I had in mind not only chafe on gear and sails, but on conflicting personalities obliged to live in close contact. Racial characteristics are probably responsible for the fact that on the whole long and severe voyage there had not been a single instance of friction aboard. The same applies to my other voyages with Polynesian or Asian crews.

It seems remarkable that Tino and Zizi, Polynesians, could stand those cold night watches in 50° S. without complaint. They always found a way to take lightly such inconveniences as snow or cold or bitter contrary gales. Instead of complaining about the weather they developed a whole string of mild jokes about it, like Tino's "Chile weather," and the "South American moon," which he hoped was not like the South American girls (it never showed itself). The whole crew had been superb—a smoothly functioning team that I was proud of, and that eased my responsibilities by showing complete confidence in me and *Varua*.

Ah You, with her background of the peaceful valley in Faaone, had the worst time of all even though she was not exposed to the weather. Seasick and probably frightened, she escaped by thinking hard about the things she loved most.

"Ropiti. Do you think the ylang-ylang tree and the *barbadine* have flowers now?" she asked me on her birthday in 50° S. during a bitter four-day gale.

The dawn was breaking over the mountains beyond the sea. To watch it I turned stiffly on my side on the hard deck, thinking how the following night I would sleep warmly in my berth—all night long and as late as I pleased. We ate a leisurely breakfast, waiting for the full light of day before we made sail. There was no hurry now although it was blowing fresh from the southwest.

I had again made a sketch from the Sailing Directions and we used it to enter. *Varua* lay over before the day's first squall as we rounded the point. We gave the kelp a good berth, thinking what a comfort to navigators this hardy plant is, wondering how many vessels it has saved in Patagonian and Magellanic waters.

On our right the small snug haven opened up, sheltered behind its hills. Beyond, we saw the mouth of the Valdivia River, disappearing around a bend into the green foothills.

LANDFALL

We hove to in the bay near a small steamer that was also waiting for the pilot.

Seafaring might be compared with a drug habit which obliges one to suffer at intervals in order to experience peaks of elation. One of these peaks is the delicious sense of anticipation when making port for the first time in a new land with its unknown people. Everything is still fresh, untasted, mysterious, and desirable. When the pilot finally came out, and went to the S.S. *Arica* instead of us, we were glad to extend the moment.

After an hour—the captain of the *Arica* had probably opened another bottle—we grew impatient, particularly since the squalls were increasing again and came down gustily off the hills. We furled sails and headed for the inner harbor under power, still using my sketch plan. In the narrows, opposite a small attractive hotel surrounded by flowers, a luxurious motor cruiser raced out loaded with people in gay holiday mood, stopped dead in the water in astonishment at sight of *Varua*. They turned and showed us in to the tiny crowded anchorage.

We drifted there, feeling our way with the sounding lead. The *Arica* came in very fast, lay practically on her beam ends as her helm was put hard over, going full speed astern and dropping her anchor at the same time. We had our first lesson in Chilean speed.

A few minutes later the pilot jumped aboard *Varua*, ordered full speed ahead. We were only about twenty-five yards from the stern of a freighter, the *Rodolfo Skalweit*.

Then: "Hard starboard let go anchor full speed astern," all in one breath.

We stopped shudderingly, sweating, a few yards to one side of the steamer, just clear of the mud flats and small fishing craft ahead and on our right. Some sort of industrial plant was half hidden beyond the steamer and the docks. Clinging to the bluff just beside us was a strange conglomeration of slumlike houses and shacks.

The pilot spoke no English except for ship handling—and that apparently limited to the commands for full speed ahead, full speed astern, hard over, and let go anchor—but we gathered from our sketchy Spanish that he would be back after noon when the tide was right to take us up the river to Valdivia where we would make formal entry.

We were alone. We sagged down on the deckhouse, blotterlike, soaking up new smells and sounds and colors. A small crowded ferryboat passed, the men with bristly little mustaches, the girls with gay scarfs around their heads. All waved and smiled friendly Latin smiles at us. Two girls and a man in a bumboat came alongside and talked to us, mostly in smiles. Everybody smiled. It was a friendly land we had come to.

The two girls and the man in the bumboat rowed ashore and went to their shack on the side of the hill right over our heads. The girl in red went in and sat by the window, looking out at us. The other girl went and picked flowers. The one in red was there whenever we looked. Later the man rowed out and handed Ah You a beautiful bouquet.

Ah You had been very quiet, eyes wide. Now suddenly she broke into tears.

"Moi avec le gros ventre. It is as if I had been to war. I never thought I would be so brave . . . just to succeed to live every day. C'est comme le paradis."

Actually, Port Corral was a pretty dreary place, but to all of us, as well as to Ah You, it was little short of paradise.

LANDFALL

Later, up the green bayou-like river, bordered by beautiful trees and green pastures, it *was* paradise.

Finally the pilot was back, with unidentified friends, or officials—in the confusion we were not quite sure which. Tino and Zizi cranked the anchor windlass with incredible speed. The anchor was barely off the bottom and I was about to back cautiously out to get well clear when the order came:

"Full speed ahead hard port."

We just missed the stern of the *Rodolfo Skalweit*, veered sharply past the channel markers, entered the narrow winding river. A fresh wind was blowing now from over the lowlands of the delta. Capitán Pratico Adolfo Montaña (he had given me his card now) looked speculatively at our impressive top hamper. His face lighted up in a big smile. He made upward gestures with his hands.

"Full sail!" was the order I gathered he wanted to make, although his training apparently began since the day of sail and the vocabulary was lacking.

"Okay, Tino, up with them," I passed the order on. Capitán Pratico Montaña's enthusiasm was infectious. Tino and Zizi looked at me incredulously, having just put in a beautiful harbor furl.

One by one the sails went up. We had entered into the spirit of the thing, cracking on sail recklessly, full speed on the engine—only hoping if we hit it would be mud.

Varua heeled, swept up the river between its narrow winding green banks, sails taut and singing in the wind that now came powerfully across green pastures and lowlands, everybody abandoned to the joy and delirium of it all.

One of the unidentified copilots lurched out of the companionway waving the guitar at Ah You. Ah You, in a red woolen jacket and ski pants, her fingers a little stiff from the cold, began to play a contagious island rhythm. Piho, unable to hold in any longer, broke into her native Paumotu dance, while up on the forward deck Tino let out a whoop and leaped into the wild *ori Tahiti* with Zizi clowning the female part. All the while speedboats full of Chileans roared downriver and fell in alongside laughing and applauding as we sailed on up the river.

The sun came out and at last there was warmth, for we had left the sea far behind.

The river widened and there were little green landings shaded by trees I had never seen before. Here and there branches of the river wound away through lush green farmland. It was like the Louisiana bayous without the moss.

Thus we came to Chile, and Valdivia. It was a fantastic introduction to a virile country. We barely got sail off in time to land with a flourish alongside a fine dock, the pilot and I temporarily buried beneath the hastily dropped mainsail. People crowded the dock and stared at us and were stared at. The officials disappeared in search of the port doctor, leaving us completely abandoned. In an hour they returned. The doctor was off in the country, or fishing, or anything— I don't know. But we were free to go and anchor in midstream and begin to let down.

Everyone from shore had gone ashore. We swung there to the river current in midstream. Vapor began to rise from the darkening water with the approach of evening.

I wanted to be alone with my thoughts: to see what *Varua* looked like after such a voyage. The pram was already in the water alongside. I rowed slowly away from *Varua* and drifted with the river.

Varua lay there on the quiet stream, framed by green hills that were already dark and indistinct in the gathering mist, so beautiful—too beautiful to have met the gales of 50° S. and come to port unscarred.

As soon as the sun had set it was cold. The mist swirled thicker over the river and blotted out the shore. Soon it would freeze at night. I knew that this was the real end of our voyage to Patagonia; the season was too far advanced to go south again on *Varua*. I might go myself, but from Valdivia *Varua* would be going north instead of south—to the warmth and sun which are her real element.

6. VALDIVIA AND THE SOUTH

Difficulties with port officials in Latin America have become so legendary that we awaited formalities with some misgiving. As it turned out, Valdivia officials did not know what to do about a yacht.

The port doctor arrived late in the evening, accompanied by two assistants who were smartly dressed in what appeared to be, respectively, military and maritime uniforms. The doctor bore the un-Latin name of Holtzapfel—the first indication we had of the strong German influence in that part of Chile. There was some confusion as to procedure, *Varua* being the first foreign yacht in their experience, but a medical release was promptly improvised and everyone settled down to a drink and a pleasant conversation with obvious relief.

In the morning, almost before we were fully awake, a launch flying a large Chilean flag came alongside. The chief of customs, formidable in a blue ankle-length Prussian army officer's coat, descended without ado into the saloon, followed by an assistant armed with a large brief case.

Here it is, I thought, shaking myself awake from the first full night's sleep in weeks, instinctively reaching for the brandy bottle and glasses in spite of the hour. Not for nothing have I received port officials in many lands.

And here it was. From the bulging brief case, which the assistant opened ceremoniously for his chief, came a formidable assortment of forms and questionnaires to be executed in Spanish, in quintuplet. There were, among others, documents entitled *Declaración de no Llevar Cargo, Lista de la Tripulación,* and *Lista de Rancho.* The prospect was appalling; and what, I wondered, did our entry have to do with a ranch. Was not, perhaps, the brusqueness of the chief merely a defense against anticipated *yanqui* bad manners?

The glasses were filled again. Ah You appeared, looking exotic in a Balinese sarong with her hair down. After introductions she retired to a corner and began to strum a piece called "Tamure" on her guitar. This was too much for Tino and Zizi, who joined in from the galley over their coffee.

Somehow, a little later, Customs Chief Señor Mucientes himself was at the saloon table with my typewriter and a stack of paper and carbons. As soon as he would finish typing a set of documents I would sign at the bottom. From the speed at which he worked and deleted, it was obvious that he was even more anxious than I to get the whole bothersome business over with. Soon we were on the last one, the *Lista de Rancho,* which turned out to be the stores list. This was quickly circumvented by writing across it the Spanish equivalent for "in ballast," after which the refilled portfolio was passed unobtrusively up on deck where it vanished for good.

From then on the meeting became less official by the minute. Piho was soon lured out into the open to do the *ori Tahiti* to Ah You's guitar. When she finally collapsed with laughter over the whole business Señor Mucientes indicated that his aide could also play—something of an understatement as we were to learn.

By the time Zizi was passing around some late breakfast, the customs assistant was singing a Spanish love song to Ah You very professionally, with the fanciest guitar accompaniment I have heard since Segovia . . . and *Varua* had a decided starboard list from the crowd on deck trying to look down the companionway and through the saloon windows at the proceedings.

It was noon when our visitors left, with warm farewells all around. It had been arranged that the customs department would declare a holiday the next day for a return engagement with more and even better talent.

Similar agreeable formalities were gone through with the port captain, Carlos Pascual Altamirano, Gobernador Marítimo, and his family; also with the local chief of the Chilean International Police, Jorge Reyes de St. Anne, and his wife.

This arrival pattern became standard routine in almost all of the Latin-American ports we visited. Our Tahitian entertainment was always matched by local talent, and official paperwork took a secondary place. Before long, however, I began to realize that I had fallen into a trap of my own setting. The social amenities involving Valdivia officials took days and days. There were visits, return visits, and later visits in order to bring friends and relatives. It was all very delightful, but we had only a limited time in which to do and see a great deal.

The only alternative, keeping relations on a strictly official level, would have meant a much more painful application of red tape; and we would have missed knowing many interesting people. In Valparaiso, a great seaport, port formalities on a purely nonsocial basis took six days, with the full-time assistance of an experienced Spanish-speaking aide from the American Consulate. We gave up the idea of stopping all along the way as we followed the coast north to Panama, for the whole procedure was required in every port, even within the same country. We decided we could use our time to better advantage by visiting a limited number of ports and using them as bases.

I must not give the impression that the Valdivia customs department exists solely for red tape, or singing and dancing. Two nights after our arrival they provided a first-hand example of the quickest police action I have ever seen. I awoke in the night to a strange sound overhead and slipped up silently through the companionway to find a dark figure crouching on deck. He saw me at almost the same instant. I caught him as he was disappearing over the side and got him down across the rail. As I turned to shout for Tino to help tie him up I saw two more shadowy figures climb over the rail on the opposite side of the ship with drawn revolvers. This, I thought, is the end. But they were reinforcements instead of enemies, in the form of customs police, and the poor robber never had a chance.

It turned out that the police, patrolling on shore, had seen our visitor surreptitiously approaching *Varua* in a small boat. With great presence of mind they had at once requisitioned a second boat and set out in pursuit, arriving a close second.

The event demonstrated graphically not only the efficiency of the Valdivia customs police, but the reason the authorities had strongly urged us to accept a guard aboard ship, which I had refused and continued to refuse on grounds of privacy. But from then on, when in port, we stripped everything movable from on deck and took other precautions against the almost invariable harbor thieves.

Preliminary formalities over with, we took *Varua* alongside a barge at the customs wharf to provision for a long stay. Watering ship was accomplished in the most delightful manner by calling out the *bomberos*—the volunteer fire department—who arrived with sirens wailing and bells clanging in a beautiful throbbing red machine that would have been any small boy's delight. They laid hose through the customs enclosure and over a couple of barges to *Varua*, and filled our tanks in record time. The friendships we made at this time, with men of the *bomberos* in their hip boots and spectacular red helmets, added a great deal to our stay in Valdivia.

We had already met the man who was to be our mentor and mainstay in Valdivia, a German shipmaster who had saved us untold embarrassment at the moment of our arrival by producing a Chilean flag. Captain Froese had retired from the sea while still young, bought land here, and prospered. During our stay he devoted himself to our problems and pleasure, and placed his nearby home completely at our disposal.

Back on her anchorage *Varua* became temporarily a houseboat on the river, a part of the strange Venice-like life of Valdivia. The main town lay on the south or left bank. The opposite shore was actually a large island, formed by a branch of the river. On this island lived and worked a part of Valdivia's mixed population, and here was located the brewery, and a shoe factory whose owners, the Rudloffs, had come to offer hospitality almost before our anchor had touched bottom. Ferryboats took the workers back and forth, and all during the day a fleet of rowboats called *botes* crossed with small groups of passengers. For the duration of our stay the *botes* all detoured to pass close to the ship for the benefit of their passengers. They also ran special *Varua* tours, and must have made a tidy sum, for the ship soon became the goal for visitors from the whole surrounding province.

At first it was all right. There were messengers with flowers from Señora Rudloff's garden; fans who had read of my

VALDIVIA AND THE SOUTH

previous voyages; kind townspeople with invitations to dinner; and high-heeled *vaqueros* from upcountry dressed in tight pants with bright sashes, boleros, and ponchos. The *vaqueros,* whose spectacular costumes made those of Hollywood cowboys seem drab, were a sensation aboard *Varua.* But as the news spread, sight-seers came in a constant parade of visiting *botes,* launches, sailboats. Some even swam out. When we went ashore we would be stopped every few feet with requests to see the ship. Finally it reached such a point that we, who had come to Chile to see, were ourselves, with our ship, such a curiosity that we had practically no time for ourselves. In the end we had to refuse visits except on Sunday.

We were living and sleeping in the saloon now, having closed off the after part of *Varua* because of the cold. Piho had her den off the galley, heated by the Shipmate range, which also helped some in the forecastle. In the morning we awoke to the whistle of Rudloff's factory and looked out on a frosty world covered with white mist as the river gave off vapors like a boiling cauldron.

By the time the Primus heater had warmed the saloon and we had finished breakfast, Captain Froese would arrive to take us ashore for errands and marketing. We would buy quantities of spectacular fruits and vegetables that never failed to astound our Tahitians. Meats were terrible, but often the fishing boats coming upriver from the sea would toss fresh *congrio* on deck as they passed, and this is one of the most delicious fish in the world.

On our first marketing expedition Ah You was exposed to her first Coca-Cola. Piho, having been in Honolulu with me, had been chanting about Coca-Colas for two days like a singing television commercial. Tahiti, for some unknown reason, is possibly the only place in the world not supplied with America's best-known export. As a matter of record, Valdivia's Coca-Colas were not very good, being amateurishly made from syrup and soda water without ice, and even Piho was disappointed.

On their first trip ashore Piho and Ah You were fascinated by the large size of the women's feet and what they took to be remarkable make-up on their legs and heels. It was, I suppose, perfectly natural for a child to notice that unhappy feature of Chilean-German female anatomy, but it had never occurred to me that neither of them was familiar with stockings. They knew all about lipstick and eyebrow pencils, but not stockings.

Tahitians are incredible in their ability to make friends in foreign lands. I had worried that they might be lonely and neglected, since they spoke no Spanish. Far from it. They were besieged. Their friends added to the piles of fruit aboard and took them ashore in the evening. Telephone numbers and addresses turned up in packages, in flowers, even in matchboxes. Sometimes the people who came to get them in the evening were better dressed than our friends —but I am not so sure about all those telephone numbers.

Even Piho had her special friend, Rosita, a handsome young Spanish woman, childless herself, who would visit Piho by the hour. I never did find out how they communicated at first, but by the time we left Piho had picked up quite a vocabulary of almost-Spanish words and expressions. The oddest sight during our stay in Valdivia was well-dressed Rosita and tumble-haired Piho sitting on the crosstrees up the mast eating grapes.

Zizi had the good fortune to become intimate with the foreman of the brewery, which led to a deviation in his behavior which continued throughout the balance of the voyage. Unlike Tino, Zizi had always been the exemplary member of our crew on other voyages. This had led to my insisting that Tino sign the Blue Cross for the duration of the voyage before leaving Tahiti. I neglected to have Zizi do so. Anyone who had known the pair previously would have been astonished if they could have seen Tino in his new role, looking with scorn, from the breathtaking eminence of his total abstinence, upon Zizi's weakness.

The Blue Cross is nothing more than signing a pledge in the presence of a Protestant church leader in Tahiti not to drink for a given period, a month, a year, several years—whatever period of time is required under the circumstances. The pledge is never broken. Considering the superficial hold which modern religion has on the Tahitians and their general disrespect for ordinary contractual obligations, the only explanation that seems reasonable is that they connect this Blue Cross thing somehow with an instinctive lingering awe of the old *tapu* system which once governed practically every act of their lives. Perhaps this is less surprising when one considers the hold that witch doctoring still has in Tahiti beneath the veneer. It is regrettable that Alcoholics Anonymous does not have such a weapon, whereby you can at the stroke of a pen turn a confirmed drunkard into a totally abstemious man for the duration, to the day, of the contract.

In the evening, to the delight of *Varua*'s crew, the riverbanks and streets as far as one could see were strung with colored lights in celebration of the founding of the city by Pedro de Valdivia in February, 1552. Valdivia must be not only one of the oldest, but also one of the most long-suffering cities in the Americas, having been wiped out by Araucanian Indians, earthquakes, and fire a half-dozen times, but always eventually rebuilt.

Chile is the melting pot of South America. A glance at the roster of national heroes reveals a list of names of most unexpected origin, including Chile's liberator and first head of state, Bernardo O'Higgins. Groups of different nationals settled in various parts of the country and are full-fledged Chileans today. Perhaps this happened because Chile was the first stop after the passage around Cape Horn in the old days and those passengers who had survived the rigors of the trip took the first opportunity to get back on solid land.

The heavy German colonization of the province of Valdivia a hundred years ago provided the impetus which led to its present importance as a commercial and agricultural center. Social life today is a strange hybrid of German culture grafted on Spanish tradition. Walking through the streets, reading signs and hearing passers-by talking, one might easily be in a town on the Rhine instead of in southern Chile. At anchor in mid-river we could smell the mountains of German pastry and *apfelstrudel* being baked on shore, and the women asked Ah You to *Kaffeeklatsches*. But when we went ashore in the evening the town became Spanish, and what appeared to be the entire population would be strolling up and down the waterfront esplanade or around the town plaza, just as in any Spanish city the world over. Dinner hour came very late; later still was the typical German band concert in the open air of the plaza. By this time it would be nearing midnight and very cold, and the music lovers would march vigorously around and around to keep warm. How the trombonists kept their fingers limber, I don't know.

Late at night when we returned to the river landing, *Varua* would be hidden in the drifting mists. The sleeping boatman would emerge from beneath his dripping poncho and row us diagonally upstream to allow for the current.

VALDIVIA AND THE SOUTH

Soon the glow of the masthead light would appear floating unattached in the air, followed moments later by the white masts themselves. Gradually *Varua* would emerge mysteriously at arm's length. The *botero* would vanish into the mist, oars creaking, his parting words hanging disembodied in the damp night air: "Buenas noches, Señor."

Valdivia is one of the rainiest ports in the world. Fortunately we were there during the best season and were only slightly hampered by the weather. As we got to know the surrounding country and its people we began to feel the life and vigor that is running through Chile today. It was a land of action and movement, although at times the movement was a bit breathtaking, for to the Chilean the thirty-mile speedboat must be driven thirty miles an hour, the seventy-mile car seventy if humanly possible. But Chile was going ahead fast, and there was the feeling in the air that she was going to succeed in becoming a great industrial nation. It was stimulating to be in a land so full of dreams—but dreams that were being converted into reality.

The only painful note was the servility of the lower classes, a result of the jealously guarded feudal system that had been practiced on the great estates for four hundred years. These vast private domains formerly controlled practically the whole country. Only recently have they begun to relinquish their grip on Chile's economy and society. In time, the new way of life, with its rising standard of living, will no doubt bring a new self-respect to the small people of Chile.

Not far from Valdivia in the Temuco region, which is also a fantastic trout-fishing paradise, we were able to see another side of the picture: the settlements of the still-proud Araucanians who were never conquered or destroyed. Farther to the north the great Inca empire crumbled before

Pizarro almost without resistance. In the far south the Patagonian Indians all but vanished. But here the little Araucanian Indians fought like tigers. When the Spanish got a foothold by means of superior weapons, and built towns, the Araucanians bided their time and drove them out again . . . and finally achieved an honorable negotiated peace. They live there today, keeping alive their old customs, proud and unique.

It was obviously too late in the season to explore the Patagonian channels with *Varua*. I did the next best thing, boarding at Puerto Montt a little steamer run by the Maritime Service of the state-owned railroad system. The *Trinidad* went about halfway to Magellan, through the inside channels and gulfs of the archipelago, visiting squall-swept island roadsteads and glass-calm estuaries that penetrated deep into the heart of the mainland between towering mountain walls.

Most of the time we were crowded like a refugee ship with a good-natured crowd that ranged from unshaven men in hip boots and what appeared to be bearskin ponchos to shivering girls in skin-tight satin dresses and exaggerated make-up, who tottered through the oil and manure of the deck on three-inch heels. Passengers who could not find room inside stood in the rain bundled in dripping ponchos. The food was bad and accommodations primitive, in particular some remarkable toilets which spouted a steady geyser of icy water two to three feet high. The only solution I could find was to undress and approach them stark naked. Obviously the trip is not for the comfort-minded tourist, but it offers unforgettable scenes ranging from the gale-swept desolation of the outer islands to the sheer grandeur of the fiords.

In sharp contrast to the passenger accommodations, the *Trinidad* operated in every other respect with astonishing speed and efficiency under a rotund little captain whose cherubic, rosy-cheeked appearance belied his exceptional ability. An odd quirk existed in the mechanical department. When the little ship was fighting strong head winds or current, the chief engineer would spray sea water all over his steaming engine with a sort of oversized Flit gun—a supplementary cooling system the engine had apparently survived for years.

The ship and her crew worked tirelessly. In one week we made thirty or forty stops, anchoring sometimes in landlocked bays in front of little unpainted wooden settlements with mud streets, sometimes off isolated homesteads where a boatload of supplies and a passenger or two would be left. To do this, we worked day and night, from island to island, threading intricate channels in the dark, routing inhabitants out at all hours with the raucous peremptory screech of our whistle. Always the shore boats would be waiting on the spot and work would begin before the ship had lost way, cargo and passengers discharging on one side, swimming livestock loading on the other. While the last of the cargo was being handled the ship would be getting under way.

We steamed hurriedly through gray rain and close channels past mile after mile of fir forests broken only by the clearings of occasional farms that were lush green from the almost perpetual mist. We crossed the Gulf of Corcovado to Melinca, which we had almost reached with *Varua*. It was not after all the southernmost inhabited port before Magellan as stated in the Sailing Directions, for we continued south via Moraleda Channel for two days of the most spectacular scenery of all, steaming at close quarters through canal-like fiords beneath towering snow-capped mountain ranges. In Moraleda Channel we met a formidable tidal bore. The others we avoided by by-passing the mouths of the gulfs.

There were wild, windy, spray-swept scenes off exposed settlements at midnight with goods and people hurtling into pitching boats and the *Trinidad* dragging in the squalls. There were peaceful interludes in landlocked coves where solid fir forests climbed steeply from water's edge into swirling black cloud masses. Usually there was icy-cold rain or mist, a phenomenon ignored by the inhabitants. It is probably responsible for the Patagonians' unusually red cheeks. When from time to time the sun broke through the churning clouds there would be dramatic scenes as the towering mountain ranges were revealed. Like the Patagonians, the *Trinidad* paid no attention to the weather, hurrying purposefully about her business, until finally we were back in Puerto Montt deeply laden with cattle, sheep, and passengers.

The voyage had been a vivid, tense, unforgettable experience, a glimpse of a new frontier in the very days of its birth. It is a raw, cruel frontier. The settlers who are opening it up, Chileans by adoption with Scandinavian, German, and Spanish blood in their veins, are certainly among the hardiest pioneers the world has ever known. Working and intermarrying with them are the island Indians whose ancestors lived there before the white man came, and who, in contrast to the natives of Magellan Straits, have managed to survive. The story will be told with pride someday, by the grandchildren of the people I saw and met down there.

Returning to Valdivia from Puerto Montt by a devious route that took me through the magnificent Andean lake country of southern Chile—traveling by bus, car, and lake steamer

VALDIVIA AND THE SOUTH

—I was so impressed by the beauty of the region that I wanted Ah You and Piho to see a little of it too. The Patagonian channel trip had been impractical for them. A comfortable week end in the mountains seemed just the thing, combining their first train ride with a chance to see beautiful lakes, snow-capped mountains, a river with waterfalls, and a little of the country itself.

Señor Jorge Reyes de St. Anne, who combined his international police duties with that of chief of Informaciónes Turísticas for Valdivia, obtained for us, in his latter capacity, round-trip excursion tickets by train to Riñihue, rail terminus of a trans-Andean route where by a remarkable combination of train, lake steamer, and car you can go over the Andes to Argentina.

The morning we left I felt that I was coming down with grippe but hated to disappoint the girls, who were breathlessly excited. The excursion turned out to be a fantastic comedy of errors which altered our whole immediate future.

The crack express connecting Santiago with the south is the equal of any of the famous trains in the United States or Europe. The lesser trains are something else again.

At Antilhue, where we were to change trains for Riñihue, we learned that the connection had been discontinued for the season. A well-meaning conductor suggested that we continue on to La Unión and change there for Lago Ranco, another Andean lake with steamer and car connection to Argentina. By the time we got to Lago Ranco hours later we found everything closed, and no steamer connection— which was just as well, for I was by then obviously sick, with fever and a violent headache.

The train rested several hours, and we ate lovely Gravenstein apples and then got aboard again and wound our way back down out of the mountains to the main line where we again changed trains after a long wait, to return to Antilhue and Valdivia. Our train was late, and crowded. As we jolted along through the night a solid rain beat against the windows, and I shook with violent chills.

The ultimate in an ill-omened day came in the form of a train wreck, as our train disputed the right of way with one from the opposite direction, fortunately at no great speed. No one was seriously hurt, but locomotives and forward cars were derailed and pointing in all directions, blocking the track quite thoroughly.

There was a long wait in the cold unheated cars and by this time I had a high fever. For some reason the rescue train which arrived after midnight stopped a half-mile down the track and all the passengers from both trains plodded soddenly through the cold rain and waited again, soaked to the skin. Eventually we reached Antilhue, changed trains again, and just at dawn clambered back aboard *Varua*.

The girls had had their train excursion. I took to my bed for two weeks with what was not grippe but a violent case of adult chicken pox complicated by pneumonia as a result of the exposure and fatigue at the onset of the fever. It was an ironical turn of fate, after the adventures of our southern voyage, to be laid low on an innocuous tourist week end.

Our attempts at isolation managed to prevent the spread of the disease to Piho and the two men, but Ah You came down with chicken pox just as I was recovering. She was still sick and in quarantine in the cabin when we called in our friends of the fire department at the end of March and watered ship for the voyage north along the Humboldt. Sadly I went to pay my respects to the port captain, and the chief of customs, and bade farewell to Captain Froese.

We would have stayed longer had it not been for the impending arrival of Mea, as we had disrespectfully taken to calling Ah You's son. Mea is a general term meaning "it" or "thing," or what have you, that the Tahitians are forever using in their conversation when too lazy to think of the right word or name. Ah You was convinced that Mea was a son—all the occult Tahitian signs clearly pointing to this fact, plus the remarkable force with which he kicked and prodded. Mea was already six and a half months old by Ah You's Oriental way of figuring. We must at all costs be in Panama within two months to allow a week or so leeway before he was due to arrive in this world.

And so, armed with the names of obstetricians all along the coast in case of emergency, we reluctantly turned our backs on Valdivia, called in full-speed-ahead Capitán Pratico Montaña with his broad, slow smile, and made a sensational descent of the river to Corral, where we left our friend and steered out into the night and the Humboldt.

7. RIVER IN THE SEA

The voyage across the southern ocean over the route of the vanished square-riggers had been the realization of a long-standing dream. We were now starting out on the second great objective of the voyage.

For years I had been fascinated by the Humboldt Current, its varied inhabitants, and its spectacular setting. On earlier voyages I had cruised its northern regions. Now, on our way to Panama from Valdivia, we were to follow its entire length. We would ride the main stream on its two-thousand-mile coastal journey to Pariñas, the westernmost point of South America, where it divides. From Pariñas we would continue along its path another thousand miles, past Ecuador and Colombia, into the Gulf of Panama. Later we would follow the Equatorial branch to the Galápagos, and on into the immensity of the Pacific until it lost its identity.

The Humboldt Current is a great river of cold water flowing through the warm Pacific. Its waters teem with such a fantastic abundance of fish and bird life that it must be seen to be believed. Antarctic sea lions, penguins, and albatross live along its route as far north as Galápagos, on the Equator itself. The coasts of Chile and Peru that are washed by the current are a strangely beautiful, utterly improbable barren desert.

Alexander von Humboldt was the first to explain the relationship between these facts. The basic food of the sea consists of microscopic marine plants or diatoms, which flourish when there is plenty of decomposed matter or detritus in the water. Humboldt realized that the cold bottom waters welling up against the continental shelf to form the current brought detritus to the surface in such profusion as to create diatom pastures unequaled elsewhere in the world, thus accounting for the vast schools of fish and the incredible flocks of birds that pursued them.

The two-thousand-mile desert coast between Valparaiso and the Gulf of Guayaquil is also due to the Humboldt, which cools the sea wind to an abnormal degree. Its temperature is then raised as it passes over the hot land, causing it to hold its moisture. Not until it reaches the top of the coastal mountains does it form condensation, and then only as fog or mist, but not rain. The great range of the Andes blocks off all chance of moisture from the other direction. Thus the coastal lands of Chile and Peru—all the length of their temperate and tropical latitudes where one would expect a green land—remain desert and fruitless unless irrigated from water sources far inland.

At first we were only conscious of the current from the miles it added to our daily run, and the increasing facility with which we drew fish from its waters. *Varua* sailed steadily north with gentle vagrant breezes, following the steep green land closely. Beyond the coastal range towered the Andes, mysterious, ever-changing. On our left the Pacific stretched its thousands of miles into infinity. Slowly the landmarks slid by one by one, with blinking lighthouses at night.

On the third day we came to the end of the rainy southland and saw the green coast give way to barren bluffs that marked the beginning of the desert coast. That night at dusk we groped our way through a maze of shipping into the inner harbor of Valparaiso where we were boarded by the doctor, who gave us pratique, asked for American cigarettes, which we did not have, and vanished into the night promising to send a pilot to berth us. For two hours we dodged steamers, launches, and craft of all descriptions, while admiring the glittering city. It was much larger than I had expected, sweeping in a great unbroken semicircle around the harbor and extending to the top of the surrounding bluffs. Tino had seen San Francisco, but for the others it was their first view of a great city. *Varua* echoed with breathless Tahitian exclamations. Ah You, almost recovered now, came and stood in the companionway wrapped in a blanket.

"Aué," she cried, "more lights than stars in the sky."

The pilot arrived, and tried distractedly and unsuccessfully to find a place to squeeze us in, finally choosing a place with no swinging room in twenty-five fathoms, which I refused.

"Why you come to Valparaiso?" he demanded accusingly, as if hoping we would go away.

Eventually we found a hole to crawl into at the head of the artificial harbor and after much backing and filling wormed our way in between two black hulls that exuded an unidentifiable odor which I later learned was whales.

With obvious relief the pilot departed—without the carton of American cigarettes and the bottle of cognac he demanded.

"Lock everything," he warned as he climbed disgustedly into his launch. "Put ropes below. Much robber here."

We locked ourselves up below with everything movable, feeling as if we were about to withstand a siege, and slept.

Our pilot's question, "Why you come to Valparaiso," was purely exasperation and required no answer. But even so, had my Spanish permitted I would have said, "To get grass to take to Tahiti," just to see his reaction to such an unlikely reply.

Actually, that was a major reason for our presence in Valparaiso. Tahiti is poor in good forage foods for its livestock, and the government agricultural service, knowing of our trip, had asked us to bring back seeds of certain new varieties from Chile and Peru with which to establish experimental pastures. These seeds were obtainable only through sources in Valparaiso and the capital, Santiago, which is reached from Valparaiso. Without this objective I would have avoided the formalities and complications of such a large seaport.

Through the kind help of Dr. Edwyn P. Reed, Director of the Fish and Game Service of Chile, and Señor Agustin Garaventa, well-known Chilean botanist, we left Valparaiso with several hundred pounds of the desired seeds, which were eventually planted in Tahiti on our return.

It was our good fortune to find that the American consul general and his wife were old friends who had been in Tahiti before the consulate there was discontinued. Through their help, and that of the personnel of the consulate, our stay was made pleasant, and the intricate port formalities accomplished as painlessly as possible.

Valparaiso was celebrating enthusiastically the day we left. We edged cautiously out of our tight berth between the two whaling vessels to the music of several brass bands. The waterfront was crowded with people waving green fronds. At first Tino and Piho took me seriously when I told them it was for our departure. Actually, it was Palm Sunday, April 6, and religion can be gay and demonstrative in South America.

We were escorted out of the harbor by the small yachts of

the Valparaiso Yacht Club, very touched by gifts of flowers and candy for the girls, and headed for the north and warmer days.

Ah You was recovered now, and Piho had miraculously escaped. *Varua* was gay with singing and more nonsense than ever as a result of the new language being spoken aboard ship.

While we had been sick in Valdivia, the other three had picked up a collection of quasi-Spanish expressions that they now threw in at the most improbable points in conversation, so that the comic bouillabaisse of pidgin English, pidgin Tahitian, and pidgin French that passed for a language aboard *Varua* was further complicated now by pidgin Spanish.

We had hoped to see Aconcagua, the highest peak in the Andes, as we sailed up the coast. It lies well inland, in the main range of the mountains, but towers nearly twenty-three thousand feet and can be seen from the sea if conditions are right. The day was beautiful. We moved under power over an unruffled sea among many little diving birds, with gulls in our rigging, and new pastel shades of color on the land, but Aconcagua remained veiled in the haze of distance. That night there was a bright moon, a land breeze full of vaguely nostalgic odors sprang up, and the decks were black with dew.

Valparaiso seemed to be the dividing line between the constantly threatening atmosphere of the south and the fair weather of the north. After three months of acrobatics that had kept us in a state of constant apprehension, the purple line that the barograph traced across its slowly revolving chart resumed the comforting regular undulation of fair-weather latitudes, high at ten o'clock, low at four, day and night.

RIVER IN THE SEA

We settled into our fair-weather routine, more delightful than ever after the severity of the southern passage. There was warmth in the sun now so I declared open season for Happy Hats. On April 9 we opened the hatches and turned out the Aladdin lamp in the saloon for the first time since entering the cold southern latitudes in early January. The chill of the Humboldt was still there at night but we knew it would burn off the next day and did not mind. When the sun was high enough to pour its slanting rays down the mountain slopes and light the cool, silently flowing waters beneath us, we could see flashing shapes of gold and emerald and sapphire waiting for our hook—that most swift and beautiful of all the fish of the sea, the *mahimahi,* or dorado, confusingly known also as dolphin but no relation to the big porpoise-like mammal of the same name. They were delicious when broiled and with them we ate real Tahitian raw fish of the finest Humboldt albacore while dreaming of swaying coconuts, rivers, and waterfalls.

Varua's brigantine rig was ideal as the breezes settled into southerly quadrants, varying a few points night and day from land to sea and back again. With squaresails lifting lazily, the ship ghosted along over the easy swells, making bubbling noises at the waterline. Every day the current grew in strength.

Day after day we followed the steep barren coast with the Andes looming indistinctly in the distance, passing one by one the historical anchorages—Coquimbo Bay, Taltal, Antofagasta, Iquique—and our excitement mounted as we neared the bird islands.

We heard them first—the throbbing swish of thousands of wings beating overhead—and as the light grew we saw them, endless columns of birds streaming past to the south from the nesting islands: San Gallán, the Ballestas, the

Chinchas, and the Independencia Bay region. Later, as the sun began to rise behind the distant Andes, they were still streaming past. I had seen it all before but this time I had the eyes of Piho and Ah You and Tino, big with wonder.

Shortly after noon we were circling close to San Gallán. An hour or so afterward we reached the Ballesta Islands. Late in the day off the Chinchas we anchored to wait for the homecoming of the birds.

As the sun neared the horizon the great Humboldt spectacle began again. The birds came winging back toward the islands. As the light began to fail they were still coming in. By dusk the islands which had been gleaming white with guano were black with birds. We lay in the quiet of the night, surrounded by the ammoniacal air of all guano islands and the throbbing that is the total of countless bird noises.

Chincha was only a preview. Our real rendezvous with the birds would be farther north. The next morning we got under way for Callao, port of Lima. The day came in very clear and we had the rare opportunity of seeing the main range of the Cordilleras extending unbroken as far as eye could reach, range mounting behind range, streaks of white mist lying in banks, and a shimmering haze rising and falling in great waves over the peaks.

Later, heading north along the coast under power in the morning calm, we were astonished and delighted to find a three-master loading guano behind Pachácamac Island.

We approached Callao with the powerful afternoon sea breeze—the virazon—on our beam, rounding San Lorenzo Island into Callao Bay under full sail, as a thousand sailing ships before us had done. At ten knots, we raced across the smooth waters of the wide sheltered bay, past another three-masted square-rigger anchored there. We went right up to the breakwater entrance where we took sail off, slipped in without a pilot, and anchored just astern of a beautiful white schooner, *Serva la Bari*. Farther in lay a fleet of yachts, and beyond, the Peruvian Yacht Club. The port doctor and officials were quick and efficient. The services and facilities of the Yacht Club were at our disposal. It was almost too good to be true.

We arrived in Callao April 17. Mea's first appearance was scheduled for the beginning of June. Since Panama was still fifteen hundred miles away it was necessary to do some careful planning.

We worked out a schedule to use our time to the best advantage. The time we had allowed for sight-seeing was over all too soon. Our Tahitians will never forget their visit to the cathedral in Lima where they stood fascinated, but trembling with fear, before the leathery brown four-hundred-year-old cadaver of Pizarro.

Most exciting of all was the trip by car across the Andes, over the fantastic Infiernillo Bridge road which is claimed by Peruvians to be "the world's highest motor road," and may well be. We climbed around precarious curves and across the trembling multiple spans of the bridge which straddles back and forth across the gorge between the mountains at 10,590-feet elevation, while far below in the river lay the wreckage of a locomotive and other heavy equipment lost during the construction days. Beyond the bridge we climbed higher and higher, past flocks of llamas, and on to the divide at Ticlio where the altimeter in the car registered well over 15,000 feet and I showed the others how to make snowballs. They could not understand why they were so weak and out of breath. We wondered if ever before Tahitians had stood on top of the Andes.

Tino sat down suddenly in the snow.

"I too old now all sudden," he said when he had a little breath again. "Too much old for mountain." He looked at Ah You and grinned.

"You stay here, Ticlio. Make baby here," he told her. "Bimeby he very very strong."

Winding our way down out of the mountains that evening we ran into a hitherto unencountered form of that great outdoor sport of Peru, wherein a pedestrian throws himself against the side of your car and simulates mortal injuries in hopes of a quick payoff. There were two cars by the side of the road, pointing in opposite directions. In the road was an apparently dead body. No one else was in sight. Our driver detoured the body and kept going as fast as possible, muttering something about "hombre malo."

I was dubious and worried about the whole thing until a half hour later, when to my utter astonishment we came upon another almost identical scene. The props were different—two small pickup trucks in this case—but the arrangement was almost exactly like the other one. I suppose both parties had seen us going up the mountain and figured we had to come down again. We never learned what the next act was.

Since the Peruvian Yacht Club had with great thoughtfulness taken care of all port formalities, we were ready to leave Callao. Our departure was less spectacular than our arrival. The virazon was all but gone and we drifted peacefully out into the evening with hardly more than steerageway. Two or three steamers converged on the harbor and lost themselves in the maze of lights. The glow of Lima, ten miles inland, radiated across the sky in a great arc. Later, the breeze came down to us from the mountains, and we slipped easily up the dark coast.

We planned to stop only once more on the mainland of Peru, at Chimbote, to see the ruins of Chan Chan, the famous private museum at Hacienda Chiclin, and the *caballitos* at Huanchaco. From Chimbote we would sail to the Lobos group.

For two days we ghosted along before light breezes over an easy swell, with bird columns streaming by in all directions and fleets of fishing cutters cruising jauntily in the teeming waters. Toward evening on the second day we approached our next destination.

Ferrol Bay is a wide expanse of water partially protected by a chain of small islands inhabited by birds and sea lions. We entered the bay between two little islands in the southern part, hunting for the sea lion rookery said to exist there, but found such furious wind squalls produced by the mountain on the southern point that we continued on across the bay and anchored at dusk off Chimbote, just inside Blanca Island. We moved uneasily to the swell but it was too late to enter the inner anchorage. Just before dark a whole fleet of little fishing boats passed very close to us, heading out to sea. When they had gone the whole bay was empty, for in spite of the splendid new half-mile-long pier jutting out from shore, and the plans of the big Corporación Peruana del Santa for the development of a coal, ore, and hydroelectric industry here, this was still just a sleepy little roadstead.

Early in the morning before the port officials were awake, I went ashore to seek influential allies to whom I had letters of introduction from Lima. When we had finished talking by long-distance phone with higher authorities up the coast at Salaverry, it was agreed that *Varua* was to be given the freedom of the port—a victory of no mean proportions. The port captain was heartbroken, for when we went to see him with the news he had already prepared at least three days' worth of red tape for us, plus written orders to "station" *Varua* in front of the Port Office, where a five-foot swell was breaking heavily on the beach.

Greatly relieved, we went back aboard and moved *Varua* to the fine shelter behind the new pier, where she would be quite safe while we were away.

At the far end of town from the pier, looking across the beautiful bay with its off-lying islands, was the fine modern Hotel Chimu, one of a string of excellent hostelries spotted unexpectedly throughout Peru. It seemed out of place here because, except for the buildings and small neat hospital of the Santa Corporation, the town of Chimbote was a gray, dusty, desert outpost. There were a few nondescript stores and frame houses in the center of town, surrounded by a collection of the most miserable dwellings imaginable, built of an incredible assortment of straw, sticks, burlap, tin, and mud. They appear to be abandoned ruins until you look closely. Then you see that they are inhabited, but habitable only through the courtesy of the Humboldt Current and the rain that never falls.

I asked my friend about the people that lived in them.

"I know some of the men that live in those places," he replied. "They make good money as fishermen."

"But why? What do they do with their money?"

"They treat themselves to several wives."

True or not, I have never seen elsewhere in civilized parts of the world, shelters as primitive as those inhabited by the working classes in many parts of Peru.

We drove up the coast to Trujillo where there is another excellent tourist hotel, past arid mountains and plains that reminded me of Arabia. The driver, as usual, kept the accelerator pushed all the way to the floor. When we passed another vehicle that was slow in making way, he would turn completely around and shrivel them with a long withering glare. All along the highway I noticed little cairns, some with makeshift crosses, and now and then a wreath. As we passed each one the driver made the Catholic sign of the cross.

"Accidents," the driver explained. "Survivors marked the spot."

"Oh," I said. "How much farther to Trujillo?"

Just beyond Trujillo, on the beach at the fishing settlement of Huanchaco, I found one of the last fleets of the reed boats called *caballitos,* "little horses." I had seen only isolated *caballitos* before, but to my delight every fisherman in Huanchaco used one.

They were friendly people who were delighted to demonstrate their little craft so that I could get pictures of them in action. Sitting or standing, they rode in on the wave crests with the ease and grace of the surfboard riders at Waikiki Beach. This was play, riding the surf for my benefit like small boys. In the more serious pursuit of their livelihood they would also run the surf to get beyond the breakers and then would paddle their little horses far on out to sea, into the heart of the Humboldt where they would use a highly perfected technique of deep-sea line fishing.

It seemed incredible that these bundles of perishable reeds would carry the rider safely to sea and back again. They are undoubtedly one of the earliest forms of watercraft known to man and have inexplicably survived unchanged down through the centuries to the present day.

Nearby were the ruins of Chan Chan, a great fortified city constructed entirely of mud bricks, that is said to have had a population of 200,000 in Inca days. From there we drove on to Hacienda Chiclin, where Señor Larco Herrera graciously showed and explained in perfect English the amazing private museum developed entirely through the efforts of this remarkable family. The collections date from four to five thousand years ago.

This was also an opportunity to see how one of the great modernized feudal plantations operated. Hacienda Chiclin is in effect a private town with a population of three thousand. All the services and functions that go to make up a town are part of the normal operation of this vast estate that grinds an average of fifteen hundred tons of sugar cane daily, six months out of the year. Señor Larco explained modestly that this was a relatively small operation, whereas the biggest plantation in this same valley grinds some five thousand tons a day every day of the year. All this, of course, is through irrigation and staggered planting that gives ripening cane throughout the year.

Exhausted by figures and facts we returned to Chimbote and *Varua* to rest and prepare for our visit to the guano islands, the main objective of this part of the voyage.

Guano is the excrement of millions of sea birds, deposited in such amazing quantities that some of the islands were built up a hundred feet and more in height. North Chincha Island, for example, was 210 feet high. When the guano had been removed it was down to 98 feet. Imagine the millions of tons of fish that countless millions of birds had to eat to add 112 feet to the elevation of an island with their droppings.

The major guano birds are the pelicans, cormorants, and boobies. The Humboldt pelican, or *alcatráz,* is a big bulky bird whose wings spread more than six feet, and who looks like a huge grotesque children's toy floating on the water. The cormorant, which is known as the *guanay*, is smaller, resembling the penguin. The *guanays* are distinctive for their beautiful flight, in endless undulating files that make one think of spring in the north and the wild geese migrating —but on a scale the wild geese never dreamed of. There are two kinds of boobies: the *piquero*, unrivaled anywhere in its spectacular diving, and the *camanay*, who has webbed feet of a violent blue and performs a most delightful mating dance.

The guano islands extend all along the Peruvian coast, directly in the path of the Humboldt Current. They are rugged and sea worn, utterly devoid of vegetation. The names were famous in the middle of the last century: Guañape, Mazorca, Chincha, San Lorenzo, Ballestas, San Gallán, Pescadores, Lobos, and many more.

The Incas had mined the guano for hundreds of years, controlling its extraction and protecting the birds. With guano and an amazing irrigation system, they turned the desert coastal slopes into fertile plantations that fed an empire.

Modern exploitation began in the 1840's. The islands were stripped of guano by hordes of slave workers. The birds were driven away or slaughtered. Scores of great square-riggers waited in precarious anchorages while the stuff was loaded into their holds; sometimes they warped their sterns close to the cliffs where it could be poured down through canvas chutes. Many ships were lost on the jagged rocks of the islands, but many more raced around the Horn with their holds full of the choking dead weight of guano, to the Chesapeake, London, or Marseilles. They lay in the harbors of a hundred ports while the crimps combed the waterfronts to snatch reluctant new crews. A sideline was the running of Chinese coolies, who would slave hopelessly on the islands with pick and shovel until the sun killed them or they committed suicide.

Fortunes were made, and during the quarter of a century the boom lasted the whole economy of Peru was built on guano . . . until the day it was gone, and with it the birds.

Eventually the islands were placed under the control of an organization formed for the purpose—the Compañia Administradora del Guano—and after one hundred years of ruthless exploitation, the present-day Peruvian put into effect the wise system of conservation that the Incas were practicing at the birth of Christ. All guano digging was stopped and the remaining birds were rigidly protected, until today they again equal the flocks of Inca days. Guano harvesting is being resumed on a small scale, with the least possible disturbance of the birds, carefully supervised and staggered to give each island plenty of chance to recover.

Today no one is allowed on the islands without a special permit. In Callao we had the pleasure of meeting the present guano administrator, Señor Carlos Llosa Belaunde, who had given us the necessary credentials.

We sailed from Chimbote in the early morning, in time to watch the departure of the birds from the nearby Santo Islands. They began to pass in large numbers as we reached the northern island, forming into a closely packed river of birds which streamed by overhead toward the northwest without a break for an hour and a quarter. Watching the spectacle from the masthead, Piho and I were so close to the birds that we could see their eyes and feel the thrust of the air beneath their wings.

We had a letter to the guardians of the Guañape Islands,

which we reached at noon. Here the natural conditions had been improved upon by a new system of artificial terracing to provide better nesting sites and aid in the accumulation of the guano. We stopped only briefly, however, because of the poor anchorage and because we were anxious to reach Lobos, still a hundred and fifty miles beyond. When the virazon began to blow in the afternoon, we made all sail and left Guañape astern.

By dawn the next day we were becalmed and went on under power through the morning haze. At noon Lobos de Afuera (Sea Lions Offshore) emerged close ahead with exactly fifty-seven fishing cutters ranged off the south point, all tailing uniformly to their anchors in the current. A little later we entered the completely landlocked inner harbor, where we found the guardian waiting in a boat, as if by mental telepathy, to indicate the best place for anchoring. From his pocket he pulled a copy of a Lima paper, *La Prensa*, with full details and photographs of *Varua* and its crew. The paper had apparently been brought over by fishermen, and the guardian had no doubt spent most of his time since then waiting for our arrival.

It was Sunday, and the guardian, Homero Paredes Basauri, took us to sit for a few minutes in the miniature church the fishermen had built on a ledge overhanging the bay. It was hardly larger than a doll house, with benches for just fourteen people. Two candles burned by the tiny altar, which was painted with primitive designs of skulls, stars, and cherubs, and decorated with miniature replicas of the crucifixion paraphernalia: hammers, plyers, ladders, and crosses.

From Homero I learned that an old friend, Enrique Marquez, was still on Lobos de Tierra. Enrique would be old now, for in 1934 he had already been lovingly caring for his lighthouse and his birds for twenty-four years. It was good to think that I would again see him, his lighthouse, and his famous tree, which was three feet high and had been there as long as men knew. Lobos de Afuera had not even one tree. The only green thing I saw was a sort of sea grass growing in the shallows of the bay.

The following morning, while Tino and Zizi went with the guardian to see the birds, and the girls hunted for seafood, I took the pram and explored the numerous coves and inlets of this favorite hideout of the buccaneers. It was the place where Dampier had careened, and lain in wait for passing Spanish ships. The anchorage is completely hidden from the sea, with exits in several directions, the island being cut in two by a narrow cleft. Warned of an approaching ship by a lookout on the hill, the buccaneers could wait to make sure what the enemy was going to do and slip out on the opposite side unobserved.

Back aboard, I got out one of my treasures, an original edition of *A New Voyage round the World* by Dampier. The buccaneers who haunted these coasts were literary men as well. The accounts they wrote, in particular those of Dampier and Woodes Rogers, are a revealing commentary on what a small group of determined men can do in the face of incredible difficulties and overwhelming odds. The story of how they warped their vessels up the fast-running river to sack Guayaquil is an almost perfect blueprint of how to do the impossible. It seemed fitting, anchored here in their favorite rendezvous, to reread the parts about Lobos and the nearby coast.

We left through the narrow canal to the southeast, passing close to the outlying rocks, which were covered with sea lions: the lobos after which these islands are named. We sailed close and heard the bellowing of the great king

RIVER IN THE SEA

bulls and the high-pitched bray of the females. Now and then, a big swell would break and the sea lions would plunge through the crest and swim offshore until the wave had receded.

Sailing through the fleet of anchored cutters we laid a course for Lobos de Tierra.

The sea region in the vicinity of the Lobos Islands is one of the most exciting places I know. Possibly the spectacular activity in the sea here is due to the acceleration of the current, and the stirring up of the bottom as the waters converge on Point Pariñas, westernmost point of South America.

We sailed through a sea red with the rich nourishment of the Humboldt. Great areas were lashed to a froth where vast schools of anchovies sought frantically to escape the jaws of the bonitos, tuna, and sea lions that pursued them, only to fall prey to the flocks of hysterically screaming birds that fell upon them from the sky. Gorged birds that had already fed rested in huge rafts on the surface or hovered overhead waiting until the process of digestion rendered them capable of rejoining the carnage. Acres of sea heaved slowly beneath the white blanket of their droppings.

The sky was filled by cruising flocks, the pelicans and *piqueros* in disordered columns and groups, the *guanays* in beautifully arranged files that spread across the heavens in rivers of closely packed birds.

Once our course took us straight through a vast thrashing school of fish being attacked by a horde of *piqueros*. This is the most spectacular sight of the Humboldt, for unlike the pelicans and the other birds who make slanting, relatively conservative dives, the *piqueros* flash like arrows straight down out of the sky in solid streams, amidst an ear-splitting din of wild cries and crackling electric excitement, miraculously missing the birds surfacing after their dives and the Antarctic gulls that hover near the surface.

The usual morning Humboldt mist lay over the sea and no land was in sight. From time to time we passed fleets of little open fishing boats with sails that resembled those of Arab dhows hanging slack waiting for the day breeze—little open boats fifty miles from shore, confident in the gentle sameness of the Humboldt weather and the dependability of the land and sea breezes.

Finally Lobos de Tierra materialized hazily out of the mirage-like atmosphere. As we drew closer we could see that the sky over the island was black with circling flocks of birds. The virazon was blowing now and we approached under sail with exhilarating speed through the smooth waters, rounded the southern rocks and coasted the eastern shore to anchor in Juanchuquita Bay not far from a stranded four-masted square-rigger, which seemed little changed in the eighteen years since I had seen it last.

My friend Enrique Marquez at once took charge, as if 1934 were yesterday, and almost before our anchor was down he had us in his boat—hurrying ashore to show us his birds. Enrique was old now; according to his reckoning he had been fifty-two years on Lobos, caring for his lighthouse and his birds. His wife was dead now, as was his tree, which had been the only tree in all the guano islands, a stunted misshapen little thing that had been there as long as one could remember. To replace his tree, Enrique now had a vine, and four geranium plants . . . and a water boat once a year to fill his reservoir and a supply boat every few months.

With the guano dust in our nostrils we trudged through scattered nesting birds to visit the great mass colonies where the different species literally cover every square inch of whole sections of the island, each kind keeping to itself. The great Juanchuquita Bay pelican colony that I remembered from 1934 had been replaced by a still larger *guanay* colony. Blue-footed boobies and *piqueros* covered a great area adjoining the guardians' headquarters and extended out of sight to the south. The birds were all around, on and all but in the buildings themselves, testifying to the gentleness of the guardians.

Later, as we sat on Enrique's porch drinking warm sweet lemonade—the late afternoon breeze heavy with guano dust—the flocks hovering overhead began to settle on the land, and in from the sea came the late fishing flocks, circling overhead in masses so dense as to throw a shadow over the island. The most beautiful sight at this time of day was the return of the *guanays,* who converged on the island in graceful streamers that extended out of sight beyond the horizon.

Soon the whole island vibrated with intense activity, throbbing movement, billowing dust clouds, as the millions of birds settled to earth, each finding the exact spot that represented home.

Later, back aboard *Varua,* clean and fresh from my shower and content after a good meal, I sat on deck with the others and looked at the island. A bright moon reflected on the glazed guano-covered ridges above the nesting areas. It was calm now and a faint air from the cooling slopes of the island carried out to us the acrid ammoniacal odor and the night cries of the birds. There was a gentle roll. In the half-light of the moon the old square-rigger seemed like a ship lying peacefully at anchor—except when one looked carefully and saw that she did not roll with the swell.

I thought of the hundreds like her that once came here, and tried to imagine what it had been like for their crews, anchored sometimes for months off the same island, living, breathing, working, eating, and sleeping with the guano always in their nostrils. I am sure they did not feel the romance and excitement we felt, visiting the islands in our own boat, able to get away from it and clean up at the end of the day, free to come and go as we pleased. But bad as their lot was on a guano voyage it was not as bad as that of the unlucky Chinese and South Sea Islanders who were brought here by deception, if not by force, to dig, and whose unmarked graves lie under the guano today.

I should like to have taken *Varua* around to the beautiful hidden anchorage at Cherra Bay, but there would not be time for that. In the cool of the morning, however, while Ah You and Piho were hunting shellfish along the beaches of Juanchuquita Bay, Enrique and I went on foot.

We stood on the jagged cliffs and looked down on the transparent sapphire and emerald waters of the jewel-like little hideaway where I had once anchored. The blue-footed boobies were still there, gravely occupied with their mating dance as if it had gone on uninterrupted since we took pictures there eighteen years ago. Down on the tiny white crescent beach at the head of the cove there was still a half-shelter where fishermen had dried their bacalao, but the fishermen were gone. In the little cove beyond, the penguins still lived, and swam close by making their soft inquisitive noises while I picked up a few shells to bring back to the girls.

We climbed to the lighthouse on the highest hill and stood on the iron platform. I could see the current sweeping past to the north like a great river, drawing from each end of the island an endless stream of foam. Up there on the horizon to the north, where we too would be going in another day, we could faintly see the tops of dark clouds, reminding me that we were nearing the limit of our two-thousand-mile rainless, squall-less sailor's paradise.

As Enrique and I walked back the long miles to Juanchuquita Bay I realized that this bone-dry sunny climate that preserves guano also preserves men's bodies, for the old man, after fifty-two years plus whatever age he was when he first came, still insisted on carrying my camera case, and could still set and keep a pace that was hard to follow.

Enrique had been keeping as a surprise for our last day the most spectacular sight of Lobos de Tierra. We passed through the *piqueros* and *guanays* of Juanchuquita Bay and climbed a rise . . . and looked down on the greatest bird colony I have ever seen: a vast sea of *guanays* that covered the whole northern end of Lobos, and which had not existed when I was there before. It was early morning and the birds had not yet gone to the fishing grounds. As far as we could see the ground was black with birds, packed body to body. As we advanced the whole mass would recoil in unison, like a vast army in retreat, raising thick dust clouds. Becoming uneasy, they began to take off in increasing clouds, casting a shadow over the island as they circled overhead before returning and landing. Finally, at about ten o'clock, they began to leave for the fishing grounds, forming into columns that streamed off in all directions—wide-flowing rivers in the air, crossing and crisscrossing, connecting us with the horizon in all directions. It was the sight with which to end our visit to the guano islands.

I went to sit once more with Enrique on the veranda overlooking his domain, bringing him a few delicacies and some photographs. Opening his heart in an impulsive gesture of intimacy he asked me into his room. The walls were completely covered with pages from newspaper rotogravure sections and magazines. On the dresser was a framed picture of his wife as a mature woman. Then, hesitating slightly, he carefully unwrapped a flat package, which I suddenly knew held all that was left of his younger days.

Slowly, one at a time, the old man showed me the faded, old-fashioned photographs. There was Enrique as a young man, all straight and lean. There was his wedding picture, with Enrique and his wife standing stiff and handsome and very solemn; and the family picture a few years later, seated, with their brood surrounding them. The photographs were all taken in a studio in Chiclayo, on the mainland, where Enrique had gone on the rare and special occasions when he had left his island.

For a long time afterward I thought of the scene—the room of this nondrinking stern old man, with its walls covered with movie stars and stills from movie extravaganzas. Was it all he had to work with, or did it represent fifty-two years of hopeless longing for something else? I wished I could talk to him and find out, but our language barrier was too great.

Enrique's boat, which had just come back loaded with fish, was waiting to take us aboard. We had to send one of the boys to shanghai Ah You and Piho, who were in their most delirious state for a long time, pants rolled up above their knees, catching crabs in the surf. They were much better than any of the men at this and came back with a sackful. Enrique insisted on giving us a few oranges which he had, a present from some fisherman friend; he had already given the girls the beautiful rare shells that were on his table.

This was another sad farewell. I suppose we will never sail this way again, although one never knows.

It was afternoon when we left Lobos de Tierra. The virazon was blowing fresh. Heeling to it with all sail set we must have looked like a pirate brigantine of Dampier's time as we rounded Cape Cross. We passed close inshore, inside of rocky Albatross Island, and I felt the swell surging beneath us just before it broke to sweep violently in and out of the caverns. We flew past the rocks at breathtaking speed, with the current funneling behind us, and the wind strong and steady. A little clan of penguins sunning themselves on a ledge well above the surf walked gravely to the precipitous edge and dove in, to appear alongside a moment later.

The sea broke and boomed through the natural arch on Albatross Island and all the sea lions lifted themselves on their flippers with their noses high in the air, swaying back and forth to see us first with one eye and then the other. A few of them dove in to swim around *Varua*, bellowing raucously each time they thrust their heads above water. We laid a course to pass Aguja Point on the mainland, thirty-five miles to the northwest. Two hours later Lobos de Tierra was an uneven fragment of yellowish fringe, just disappearing over the horizon astern.

The next morning, having made fabulous time during the night, we passed Point Pariñas. A little later we encountered several sailing balsa rafts like those used by the Incas, and then entered the snug little harbor of Talara to get fresh supplies for the last long leg of our voyage to Panama.

We were off again at dawn, for there was no time to waste now with a thousand miles still to go and Ah You's baby due in less than a month. We were leaving the main stream of the Humboldt and following the northern branch to Panama. Later we would return and rejoin it on its last sweep through Galápagos and on until it loses itself in the vast Pacific. We had fuel enough to use power all the way to Panama if the winds failed us.

As we cast off from the big mooring buoys, the jaunty little fishing cutters of the Talara fleet were making sail around us, and we all went out together. The land breeze was still blowing fresh from the southeast. We slanted away up the coast for Cape Blanco under full sail. Later, as the sun grew hot, the breeze worked through south to southwest. Off Cape Blanco we passed another fleet of native fishing boats and a few sport fishermen with pulpits on the bowsprit and rods over the stern—out for the great game fish that abound where the current meets the waters from the Gulf of Guayaquil.

We left the barren headland with its forest of oil derricks along the ridge and headed on across the gulf. When we sighted the land again on the Ecuador side it was violent green in color—for we had at last left the desert coast behind. From now on we would have the tropical rain forest and mangrove shores to follow, but we stayed well out to avoid counter-eddies near shore, and so as to keep in the north-going branch of the Humboldt. Piho discovered that we were entering another kind of world, and was all excited when I came up on deck after a nap.

"I saw other kind bird today," she announced. "This kind air bird, not water bird." This meant that she had begun to see land birds or perhaps the more familiar high-flying sea birds of her previous experience, instead of the guano birds we had been with for so long.

La Plata Island, Cape San Lorenzo and other familiar landmarks slipped by. The breezes were still fair but light and shifting; our square rig lifted us gently but steadily on our course. With the breeze astern it was really hot, for we were under the Equator now. We rigged an awning for the helmsman and threw buckets of water on ourselves and the deck.

On the third day a lovely soft dawn revealed the shadowy outline of Cape San Francisco on the seemingly endless coast we occasionally glimpsed. We were nearing the border of Ecuador and Colombia. It was a joy to be warm all the time, even at night. I went with relish to my dawn watch, and when the day broke everyone was on deck to help paint and varnish before the famous Panama rainy season. *Varua* must look her best when we got to port.

I got out the Sailing Directions and reread that much-quoted paragraph in which the navigation of the approaches to the Gulf of Panama in a sailing vessel is said to be "one of the most tedious, uncertain, and vexatious undertakings known to the seaman." But with our tanks full of diesel oil and our dependable auxiliary engine, I could take only perverse pleasure in the fact that statements of this sort still appear in the directions.

We sailed on. The breeze freshened and worked into the west at noon. We saw turtles, *mahimahi,* and flying fish; overhead our first man-of-war bird soared in great wheeling circles. There was still no rain. But as night fell the land was piled with high black clouds, the first we had seen since south of Valparaiso. Our fair wind died out. We went on under power.

Dawn came again and we were still under power and there was a beautiful *mahimahi* on our line fighting hard. He dropped to the deck from a broken hook, all flashing yellow and gold. Tino and I had all we could do to capture him before he could leap overboard again, while Piho, hair flying loose in the first breeze of day, shouted directions. Piho should have been a chiefess two hundred years ago, with her predilection for command.

We were off Colombia now, not far from the mouths of the Rio Mira Delta. The rivers were in flood from heavy rains, which we could see sweeping the low coast and the hills beyond. Where the yellow floodwaters met the blue of the current they were cut off squarely and abruptly.

We had been following our river in the sea for three thousand miles. Along the dry coasts of Chile and Peru it had flowed silently, invisibly—revealing its presence by the boost it gave our daily runs. Now, with the flooding yellow river waters to give it a clear line of demarcation, it was suddenly and dramatically visible.

Along the edge of the two waters lay an unbroken line of debris which was a natural aquarium inhabited by countless small sea creatures. Flashing *mahimahi* dolphins waited impatiently for unwary small fish to stray from their shelter. Surely, we thought, there is no more beautiful fish in the sea than the dolphin. There were leaping rays, mating turtles, big and little whales. We even saw crabs and snakes.

All day we followed our blue river, staying in the clear water just outside the line of flotsam. At noon there was again a fine breeze from the west and we made sail and stopped the engine. Later we passed Gorgona Island, well offshore, still following the amazing line of debris with its seething life. We saw several more dolphin all together, idling in the shelter of a great green-leaved floating jungle tree. There were more leaping rays and feeding bonitos and diving birds until suddenly a gigantic gray-black shark cruised slowly by and everything else had vanished.

"Voilà la police," shouted Tino.

The excitement of it all was kept alive by the speed of

our sailing, and by the running-rapids noise where the blue water flowed past the yellow flood.

At night we worked a little to the west to keep out of the debris. We were approaching Panama, and the crew were talking of reaching Tahiti already. At last, at midnight, the rain worked out from the land and enveloped us, a strange sensation after so long a time. At dawn when Piho came on deck it was still raining.

"Aué tatou é! Te ua! Rain! Plui! Agua!" she screamed with joy in four languages, and jumped into a puddle in the sagging canvas trough I had prepared for her, rolling and squirming in it like a young seal.

We worked in again to the edge of our blue river and repeated the previous days' entertainments. We were off Buenaventura now. A coastal steamer heading in to port was a good check on our dead reckoning. Again we were under power, for the rain had killed our breeze. There were bird rafts on the calm sea.

"What other kind bird this, Piho?" I asked her in jest.

"This one boat bird," she replied at once.

This was a coast of many rivers. We were now off the Rio San Juan Delta and our line of flotsam was thicker than ever. Then came Cape Corrientes, so hard to round when you are southbound, with its domelike hills standing out sharply in the clear atmosphere.

The next day we were still under power without a breath of wind, but squalls were working in from the northwest. The first one came while I was below eating breakfast, with Ah You, clad in a *pareu*, at the wheel. It struck with a blast of wind and cold rain. Thinking of Mea, I rushed up to get Ah You out of the rain, and found her in ecstasy.

"Mais non! It is wonderful," she cried, as Piho came rushing aft with a bucketful she had already collected from the scuppers and poured it over herself and Ah You amidst peals of delighted laughter.

I threw up my hands and returned to breakfast but before I could get a mouthful the engine-room bell clanged loudly in the emergency signal from the wheel. Again I rushed on deck.

Both girls were screaming *"Mahimahi"* and pointing to our line.

It was a big male dolphin that threw the wire leader around my neck as I was swinging him over the rail. Fortunately for me the hook came out of his mouth at the same time and he fell back into the sea. Secretly I was glad, for I hate to catch these lovely creatures. But I realized that I could have disappeared without trace if I had been alone on deck, and if the hook had not come out of his mouth.

I cleared the line, and when a few yards were out a fine tuna took it; but the frantic zigzag track told what was going to happen even before we saw the black fin of the shark cutting the water just behind. There was a flash and half the tuna was gone, but there was plenty left for us. I put the line over again, just to get the kinks out before coiling it to hang up. In an instant another tuna was on the hook, and on deck, whole. We spent a half hour washing off the blood which had spurted from the amputated tuna all over me and Ah You and *Varua*. The downpour, forgotten during the excitement, was still going on.

Ah You must be frozen by now, I thought, and again tried to get her to go below. The rain was running in a stream off the tip of her nose.

"Mais non. C'est bon." She looked at me puzzled. "C'est bon, c'est bon, c'est bon" . . . and both girls started singing the French song *"C'est si Bon,"* which had been popular in Tahiti before we left.

Varua off Tahiti

Ah You

Zizi and Piho with dorado

The author in *Varua*'s saloon

Tino

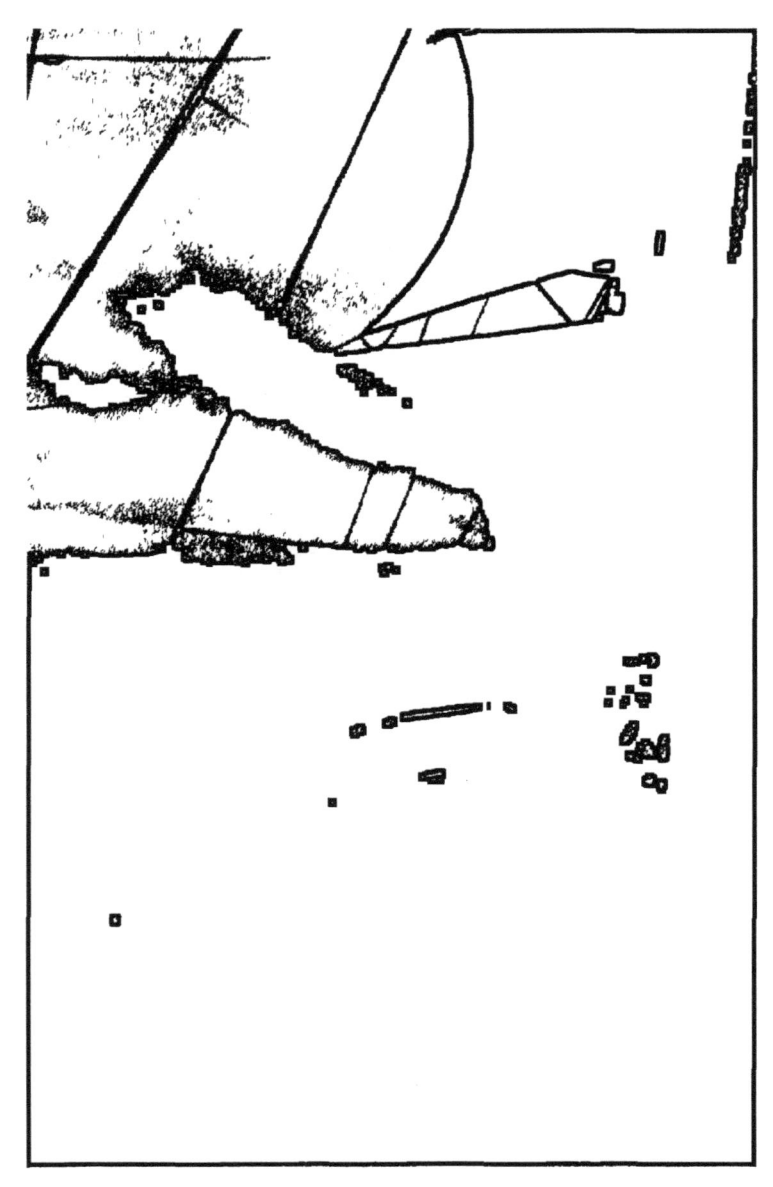

Varua's sails etched against a graying sky

Varua drives south against unexpected head winds

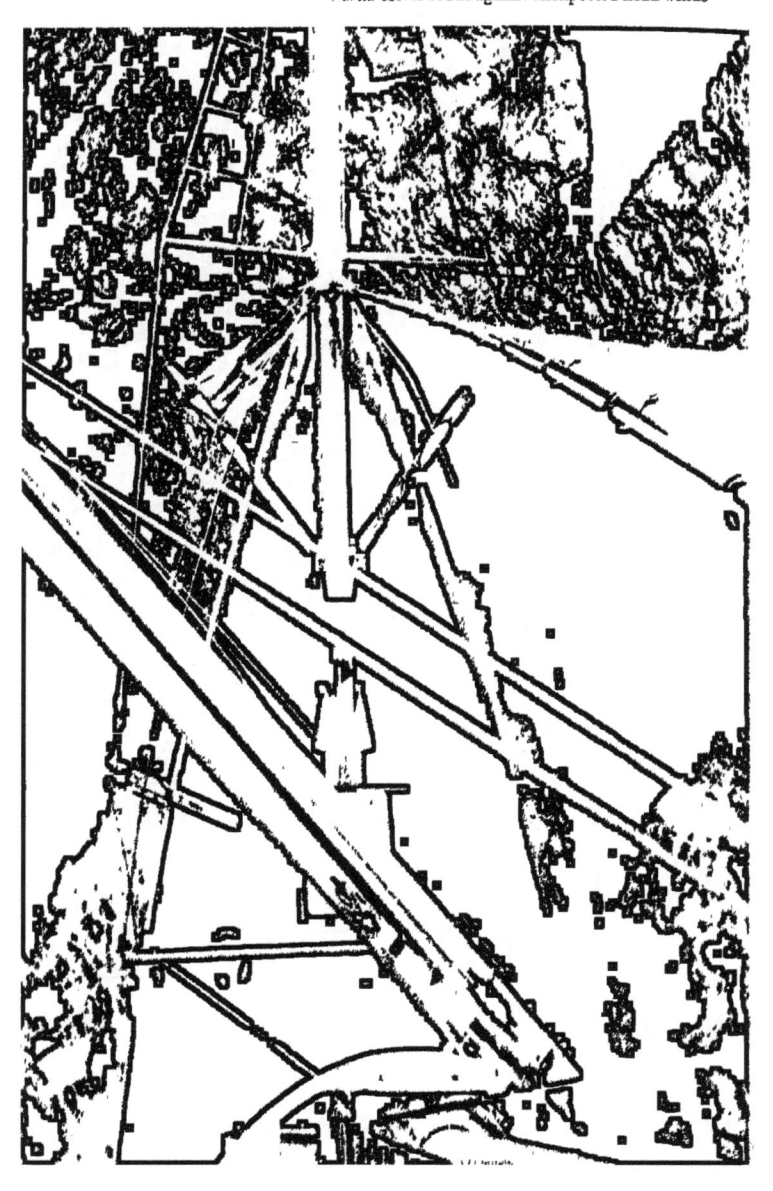

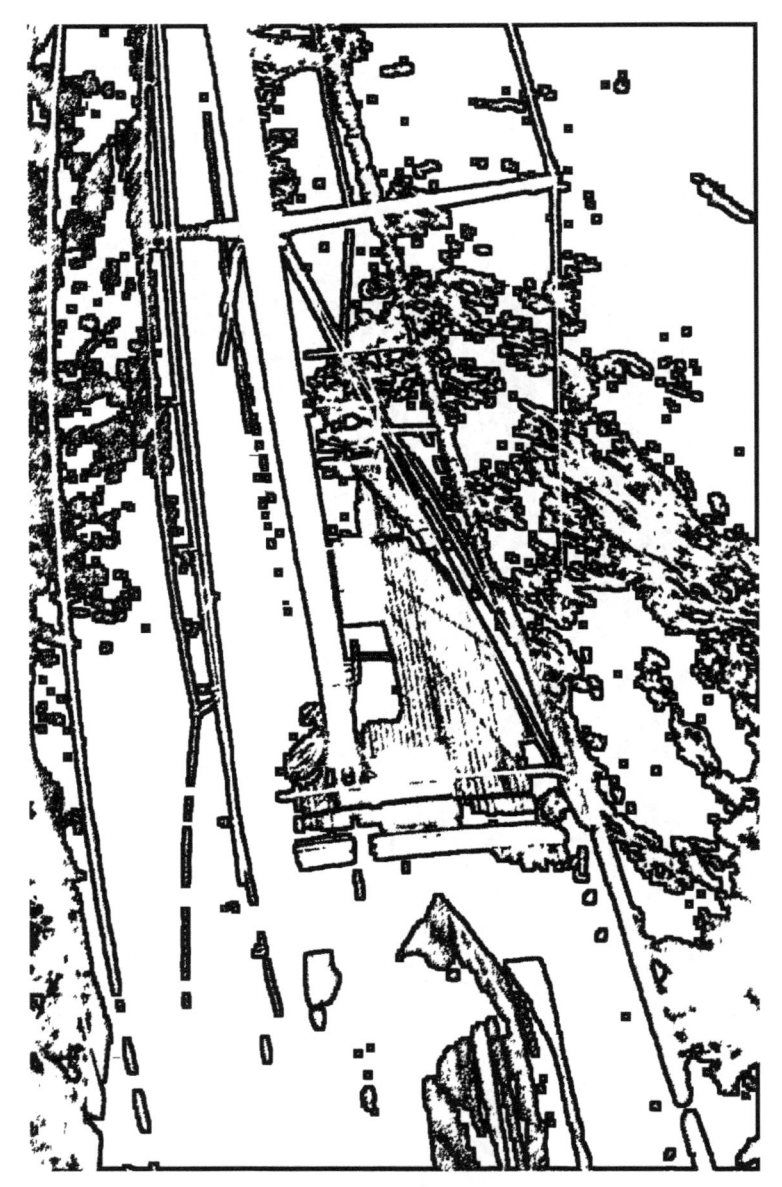

Close hauled, *Varua* leaves Panama

Varua sails upriver to Valdivia with pilot aboard

Varua at rest, Valdivia

Fishermen of Huanchaco with *caballitos*

Fishermen's miniature church, Lobos de Afuera

Enrique shows his birds to Ah You and Piho

Hina in her basket at the foot of the mainmast

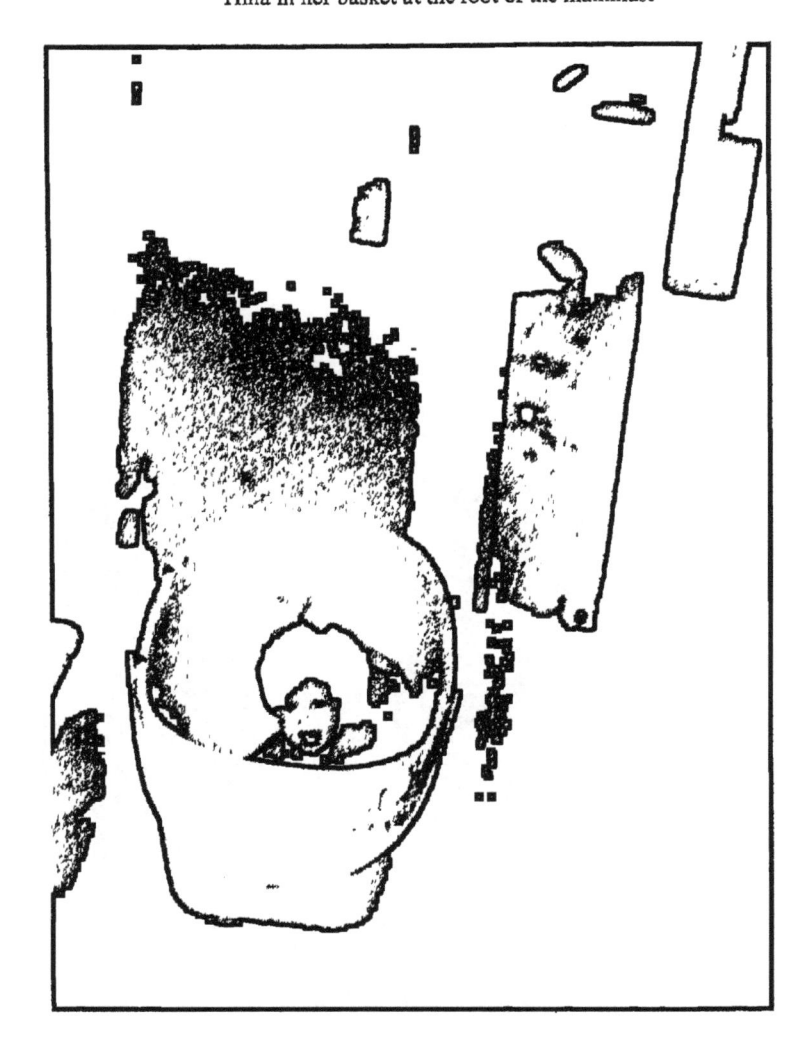

Hina and Ah You at the penguin village, Elizabeth Bay, Galápagos

Tino and the belligerent sea lion, Galápagos

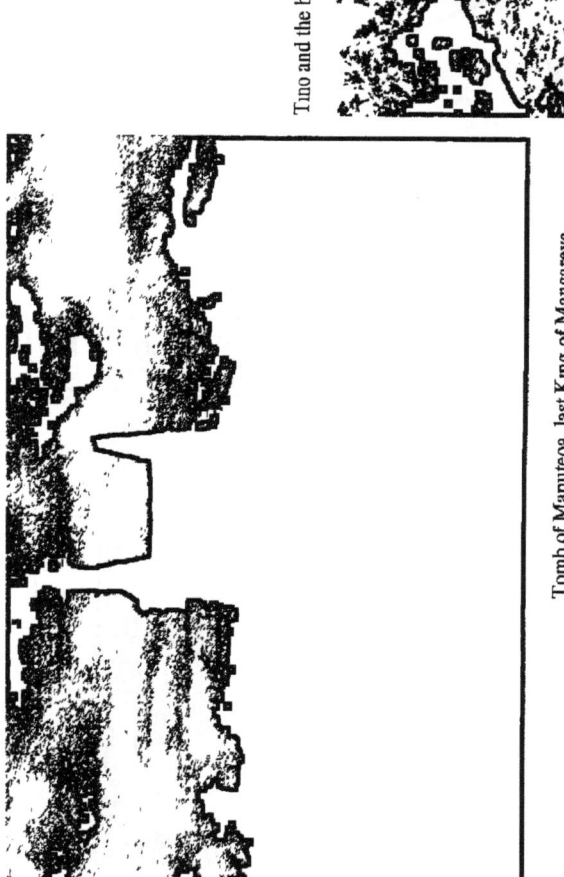

Tomb of Maputeoa, last King of Mangareva

Everything furled and under power for the calm of the last three hundred miles

Approaching Tahiti at the end of the voyage

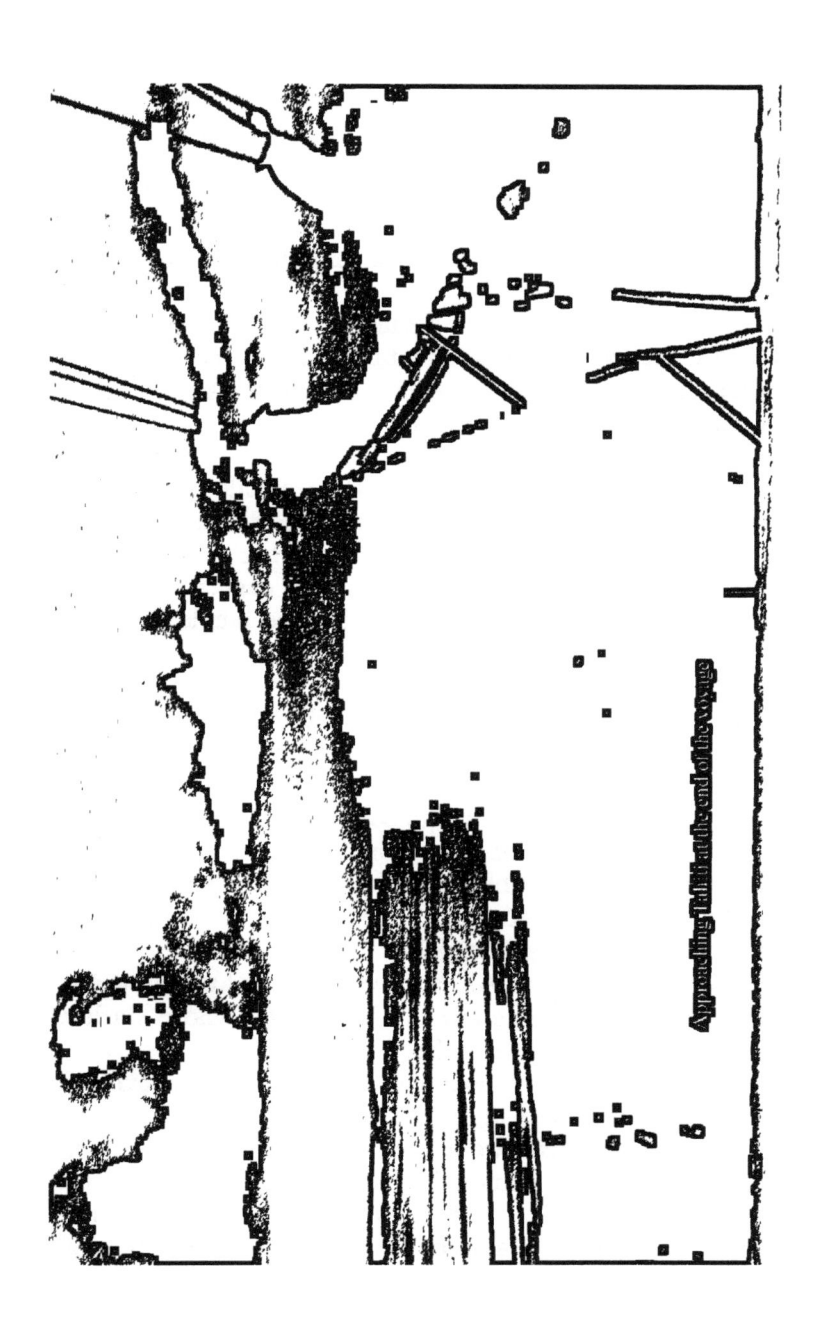

RIVER IN THE SEA

The trouble with me was that I kept forgetting that all Tahitians, and apparently adopted Tahitians of Chinese-Siamese ancestry as well, are never happier than when they are out in the rain.

When the squall was over we made sail to the new breeze. The atmosphere was now unnaturally clear and the whole Colombian coast stood out, etched against the sky. At noon we passed four tuna clippers at work.

Another night . . . and another dawn. We were off a wooded green promontory, with white clouds lying in the lower valleys like glaciers. Behind rose the perpetually rain-drenched peak of Cerro Sapo, on the other side of which flows the unruly River Sambu that on an earlier voyage, in a flash flood, threw my ship deep into the jungle. Panama was only a day's sail now.

Mea still had a good two weeks to go, so we detoured through the Pearl Islands, coasting leisurely all day along the luxurious shores, stretching out the joy of arrival. As we approached Rey Island, the first of the group, the Tahitians had a contest going to see who could find things first. They identified branches and leaves in the water, and trees on shore I could not possibly recognize at that distance.

"Aiaaaa," screamed Piho. "Coco-coco-coco-coco!" She had seen the first coconut palm.

A little later it was Ah You who cried "Aué tatou é—Tipané!" as she recognized the frangipani, whose starlike flowers she likes to wear in her hair.

"The island is like a bouquet," she added, unbelievingly. "A bouquet of flowers in the sea."

As we came closer we saw many trees with white blossoms that we did not know but which made us think of the Paumotu *tafano* . . . and spontaneously they were suddenly all singing the Paumotu song to the *tafano* in the soft

Tahitian harmony—Tino's deep warm bass complimenting the high youthful ones of Piho and Ah You.

It was glassy calm now. Over on the Panama side of the gulf were two schooner-rigged *cayucas,* no doubt bringing plantains from Garachiné. If we had been closer we would have seen the multipatched sails and shredded rigging. From *Varua* the Panama coast looked like a series of blue-green islands with occasional white clouds arranged over the more important ones. My Tahitians were trying the impossible task of calculating how many miles it was, and how many days of sailing since they saw a green land.

"Comme c'est vert," they kept repeating. "How green it is."

These last few days had been paradise sailing, except for the lack of wind at times. There were many moments I would remember, like this last morning before dawn at the masthead with Piho, looking for Trollope Light, with the gleaming white yards beneath us and the slender hull making stars in the water under the bow while the porpoises left fiery trails all around.

Shortly after noon we anchored by two little round islets with a spit of white sand between them on which to bathe at sunset, but when we came back to swim there after exploring the shores in the pram the spit had vanished under many feet of emerald water. I had forgotten the big Panama tides. So instead, we made a raid on the palms for coconuts, and collected some perfumed berries and a boatload of flowers.

One more day and by midafternoon we were off Taboga. We could see Balboa and the canal entrance. Since it was too late to enter, we anchored off Taboga village, trying to remain invisible but flying the quarantine flag just in case. Tino tried his Spanish on the boatmen.

"Amigo," he shouted, with a voice of authority, "you bring mangoes, avocats—pronto. Claro. Claaro!"

Tino's lingual improvisations seemed both to confuse and energize strangers; almost invariably they got results. In no time we had our mangoes, and avocados, and a few more fruits thrown in for good measure. And the boatman refused to take money!

In the evening there was the perfume in the night wind which I had never forgotten, for Taboga was the first place I discovered it long ago.

We were still painting *Varua*. By evening we had finished all we could do, and she gleamed from stem to stern, and we were content and proud as we sat on deck looking at the sights. The Tahitians stared unbelievingly at the flashing lights of planes in the sky every few minutes instead of once a month as at home. All the while a procession of steamers festooned with lights emerged from the Pacific end of the canal and headed out into the night. Over all the canal region there was a glow in the sky even bigger than that over Valparaiso or Lima. No one slept very much and, before we knew it, it was dawn.

We joined the never-ending procession of ships from the world over, still trying to remain invisible so that we could get to the Balboa Yacht Club without a pilot. But a boarding party caught us when we were only a few hundred yards from our goal and apologetically asked us to wait for the pilot. We could have found our mooring alone; but it was the regulation.

The pilot too was apologetic and let me bring *Varua* in the rest of the way while he gave us the latest news. The outer pair of mooring buoys seemed to have been waiting specifically for *Varua* to come. We moored bow and stern, just beside the main ship canal. Everything was familiar and comforting. We had sailed 8,662 miles since we left Tahiti. We were due for a long rest, and this was the place.

8. PANAMA AND THE NEW APPRENTICE

As soon as we were moored off Balboa, we went to the prenatal clinic in the maternity ward of Gorgas Hospital. Since Ah You speaks no English, I told her to sit down while I registered for her and answered the usual questions. I was the only man in sight.

I found myself at the end of a waiting line of very pregnant women, instinctively holding in my stomach. The women ahead of me were talking in stage whispers and it was impossible not to eavesdrop. There was much comparing of weights and diets and related shop talk.

The line moved along slowly. When I got to the desk I handed Ah You's entry card to the attractive starched nurse there who without looking up began to call me "Mrs. Robinson" and started writing down the answers to questions. About the third question she looked up, started, and gasped in utter confusion.

I explained and pointed to Ah You sitting in the corner, trying to look invisible. The other nurses came to join in the excitement of this intrusion from the South Seas and it was some time before the assembly-line efficiency of the clinic was restored. It was obvious that Ah You was going to be the pet of the maternity ward.

Back aboard *Varua* Ah You and I settled down to await Mea's appearance. There was time to renew old friendships and pay sentimental visits to the scenes of my other voyages.

Panama has been the base for some of the most exciting adventures of my life and it is like homecoming when I return.

Ah You, Piho, and the two men were introduced to chrome and glass supermarkets, cinema palaces, cabaret night life, Constellations, air conditioning, and the almost aseptic cleanliness of the Canal Zone. The latter impressed Zizi tremendously. I think he was secretly horrified at the idea and would be glad when he could escape such a depressing environment.

Sad to say, the people of *Varua* also learned about the color line in the Canal Zone—something of an experience for proud Polynesians. The line was less distinct than before, but still apparent. Curiously enough it applied only to Tino and Zizi. When I tried to explain this hitherto unmet problem to them they looked uncomprehending but cooperative as always.

Mea arrived on schedule to the surprise of everyone including the doctors, who had doubted that Ah You's modest bulge concealed a nine-month-old son. The general opinion was that the whole thing was a Tahitian miscalculation.

The night it happened Ah You forgot to mention the matter to me until almost the last minute. Such casualness is apparently a typical Tahitian attitude, as I was again reminded just the other day when Moeline, the girl who helps with the housework in Paea, had her baby. On Friday Moeline got in a good day's work. Just before dawn on Saturday morning she got up, careful not to awaken us, and bicycled down the road to her family home, where she promptly had her baby. On Tuesday morning she was back on her bicycle wanting to return to work.

Ah You did not have to go on a bicycle, because Dr. Arias sent a luxurious ambulance the minute we phoned. She had been making photographic enlargements with me until midnight. Not until we had finished did she think to mention that things had started several hours before and that perhaps we ought to go to the hospital right away.

To Ah You's astonishment and disbelief—and my secret delight—Mea was a girl, with long black hair like her mother. In a few days she came home to *Varua* where she lived in a beautiful basket given us by my oldest friends in Panama. She was named Hina Mareva Robinson.

It was a long time before Ah You stopped being teased about the complete breakdown of her Tahitian forecasting service; and for quite a while the name Mea clung, and we made slips of the tongue and referred to Hina as he.

When Hina was two weeks old and everything under control, I flew to New England, leaving *Varua* and its little clan under the watchful eye of the Yacht Club and Lieutenant Feeney.

Lieutenant Feeney had been with the boarding party as Naval Intelligence officer on our arrival, and had been back several times in the first days full of interest. I thought he had been delegated to keep an eye on *Varua* and her strangely assorted crew. But after he fell down the Yacht Club gangway while bringing us an enormous record player to use while ours was being repaired, and went to have five stitches taken in his chin, and then came back with the miraculously undamaged machine—I decided that his interest in *Varua* was beyond the line of duty.

Lieutenant Feeney and his wife turned out to be delightful friends, keeping open house for all of us, and lending us their jalopy for shopping expeditions. Since the Feeneys had bought a dachshund puppy instead of a new generator, the car had to be parked on an incline in order to be started, but fortunately Balboa has numerous hills.

On my return from New England, Carlos, a good Colombian mechanic, came to help me overhaul *Varua*'s engine which had completed a long period of faithful service. Tino and Zizi worked on sails and rigging, putting everything in perfect shape for the voyage to Tahiti.

The days passed quickly. At seven every morning a whistle over in Panama City, exactly like the one at Rudloff's shoe factory, made us think of our friends in Valdivia, and appreciate how much warmer we now were. Panama is hot and moist, but on our mooring off the Yacht Club we got the sea breeze from across Panama Bay, and our big full-length awnings protected us from the frequent showers which we could see forming over Balboa Heights and Ancon. We would eat our meals on deck, watching the incredible procession of ships from the ends of the earth passing almost within arm's length of us.

Varua was like a houseboat at a great world crossroads. But unlike a houseboat she could join that procession of ships and go anywhere they could go and a lot of places they couldn't, so that our lives were filled with the feeling of freedom. It is the same in Tahiti, where our home is really just a spacious thatch-covered terrace where one lives practically outdoors with the birds and flowers, while beyond the lawn the blue Pacific stretches to infinity.

In the States I had felt uneasy and stifled within the unaccustomed confines of narrow house walls and hemmed-in streets. This was one of the things I had to try to explain on my return, when the girls were asking what it had been like up there and why anyone who could live in the wonderful land of America did not do so. Fortunately most of the questions were easier to answer than that one.

No, I would tell them, the men don't all wear white suits and probably not one in a million owns a *pareu* or knows what one is. Most of them are embarrassed to be seen holding and feeding babies, and grandmothers are not commonly seen riding motorcycles.

And, I told Piho for the hundredth time, North America is not an island with a reef around it.

"Do they smile at you much?" Ah You wanted to know, and I had to tell her that the people on the street rarely smiled because they were apt to be preoccupied.

"And they all hurry along the street very fast," I went on, having read this in a book. "Not like in Papeete and here in Panama City where everybody has plenty of time."

"But that is just the way you do!" She looked amused, and went on to describe how she and Piho would recognize me in the crowd at Valparaiso from across the harbor. They would see one figure walking much faster than anyone else and they would tell Tino, "C'est monsieur; go get him in the boat."

Probably the most surprising thing I learned about *Varua*'s crew during our stay was that, outside of Zizi, who spent his evenings ashore drinking beer, they were content, once they had seen the night life and the general layout of the city, to return to their more simple pleasures of fishing over the side, singing with the guitar, or just talking.

"There is so much to do in Tahiti," they would say, "the reef, the rivers, the valleys, the tour de l'ile. Here we can't do that."

"Patience," I would tell them. "It won't be long now."

Tino was never happier than when he was allowed to stay aboard and baby-sit. This was a break for us since the sitters from shore all got seasick from the movement of *Varua* when the ships went by in the canal. When we had to take Tino ashore for some special occasion we called in the widely talented and ever-faithful Lieutenant Feeney himself and knew that Hina was in the best possible hands.

Before leaving the Canal Zone we were to visit Barro Colorado Island, a side trip which in addition to its main objective would take us through the most interesting half of the canal itself. Barro Colorado is a large section of tropical rain jungle that became an island when the Chagres River was dammed to form Gatun Lake, which furnishes the water for the great locks at both ends of the canal. It is complete with all the denizens of the jungle who were living there originally as well as others who fled there when the rising waters flooded the surrounding lowlands. The island was made a permanent botanical and wild life sanctuary and has been for many years under the devoted care of Dr. James Zetek of the Smithsonian Institution.

Naturalists come to Barro Colorado from all over the world to study the wild life in its natural setting, their work facilitated by excellent trails and observation posts, and by the fact that everything is concentrated within the limits of an island. Other research requiring tropical conditions is also carried out from time to time, such as termite control investigations and experiments by Eastman Kodak Company.

Because of our plant collecting, permission was granted for *Varua* to visit the island. When arrangements had been made we transited the canal through the Pedro Miguel and Miraflores locks into Gatun Lake. A bayou-like side channel leads through the still-visible skeletons of drowned jungle trees to Barro Colorado. We anchored there in a tranquil dead end, surrounded on three sides by the dense green jungle.

Twice a week the Barro Colorado launch wove its way

through the dead treetops, across the ship canal, and up another bayou-like waterway on the opposite side to Frijoles, an abandoned station on the transisthmian railway. Frijoles, of course, is Spanish for beans, a not unsuitable name for this deserted way station dating from the construction days. There Dr. Zetek would arrive on the morning train from Balboa with a thin little crowd of paying visitors, for this able scientist, who should be allowed to spend his time to better advantage, has bowed to the necessity of collecting funds wherever he can to bolster up his meager budget. His personally conducted tours give visitors a chance to see Barro Colorado, consume one of the doctor's Barro Colorado Special cocktails and an excellent lunch, after which they listen to a humorously informative talk before returning to Frijoles for the late afternoon train.

We spent ten days there anchored off Dr. Zetek's private jungle. At dawn we would be awakened by the howling of the Mono Negra monkeys, whose lionlike voices far outstrip their size and daring. We collected plants and seeds that might be successful in Tahiti, and followed the jungle trails accompanied by Chi Chi, the guardian. Most of the time the effect of the natural halflight of the forest was heightened by the almost perpetually threatening skies of the rainy season. The wild inhabitants seemed to be reasonably friendly and not too concerned at being spied upon as they went about their daily lives.

In the clearing by the headquarters buildings there were almost always tame deer, pet coati-mundis, and butterflies like flying six-inch hibiscus blossoms.

The island also shelters some of Central America's most deadly snakes. There has never been an accident, but the big fer-de-lance coiled up in alcohol on Dr. Zetek's table was caught at the boat landing. I am just as glad that we encountered no living specimens. We did, however, fish a strange half-drowned animal out of the lake one day as he drifted past *Varua* clinging to a bit of wood. He turned out to be an adult three-toed sloth, a beast that seems to be a direct link with prehistoric times. Even his terrifying experience failed to disturb his painfully deliberate slow motion. As soon as he had recovered his breath he suspended himself upside down from the boom to dry out and sleep all day. He suffered from moths in his fur, which his immersion had failed to dislodge. I was tempted to sprinkle him with DDT but desisted, fearing to upset the balance of nature. That evening we put him ashore safely on a nice jungle point of the island.

The nights at Barro Colorado were filled with a cacophony of unidentified cries, howls, and screams, as the nocturnal creatures carried on their ceaseless struggle for existence. Only a hundred yards or so away, the ships moved silently past the island, ablaze with lights on the calm black waters of the canal.

Tino, who is afraid of nothing on the sea, was so intimidated by the animal cries and the snake stories that he preferred to stay aboard *Varua* the whole time.

On August 1 a launch brought the pilot aboard and we locked down to sea level again for a few last days at our mooring off the Yacht Club. The fresh waters of Gatun Lake had removed most of the growth on our bottom, but that was not enough. We put *Varua* on the beach at Far Fan, across the canal from Balboa, and gave her bottom two coats of antifouling paint. After that we collected our last plants from the Botanical Gardens at Summit, got our stores aboard, and were ready to sail. Hina was two months old now, which we felt was a good age to go to sea.

PANAMA AND THE NEW APPRENTICE

When I went to the Port Office for my sailing papers I came back with an officially registered addition to our crew: "Hina Robinson, Apprentice. Age two months. Weight nine pounds." And so the crew list sounded more than ever like the cast of a Disney movie: Piho, Tino, Hina, Zizi, and Philo, as everyone but me called Ah You.

The back of the logbook was full of notes in three languages about baby feeding in case Nature failed, and our ships stores contained many items for the exclusive use of our new apprentice, the most conspicuous of which was an incredible number of bales of disposable diapers that filled practically all the free space below decks.

The day before sailing we went alongside the Yacht Club landing to fill tanks, and lay there the last night with *Varua* looking most mysterious and romantic under the glare of a solitary floodlight.

In the morning Piho was noisily fishing from the dock for what she referred to as "triple fins" with a small boy acquaintance. She abandoned that occupation at once when I sent her for a last time to get all the ice cream we all could eat, our last American ice cream.

It had been good to gorge ourselves on this and all the other luxuries which are commonplace to Americans but unavailable in Tahiti. It was good, as well, to shop in the incredible supermarkets with their chrome and glass cleanliness, instead of the poorly stocked dusty stores and fly-ridden market in Papeete. The different scale of living enjoyed by Americans was brought home to me one day when little Harold Feeney, Jr., and another child were aboard. I asked them to have some of our ice cream and Coca-Cola, an invitation that would have caused a near-riot in Tahiti.

"No thanks," replied the children. "We have lots at home."

It had been a joy to watch the girls react to all the new sights and sensations, and walk big-eyed through the air-conditioned stores filled with unheard-of wonders, while I felt as if I personally were responsible for it all. I had had some doubts as to the wisdom of letting them see all this in case they would pine for it later, but my mind was put at ease by a remark from Ah You when we were returning from our last trip ashore.

"It has all been wonderful," she said. "Cape Horn . . . Chile . . . snow on the Andes . . . Panama most of all because it is green and hot and it rains like in Tahiti. But the greatest pleasure is the valley at home at Ofaipapa and the flowers, and I would like to pull some weeds in the lawn."

"What was best of all?" I asked her.

"My room in the hospital," she replied without hesitation. "And the sweet nurses who brought me things all day long and did things for me as if I were a queen. I should like to have stayed there longer if it had been possible."

Our stay in Panama had been calm, relaxing, and gratifying; but now, sated with good things, we were eager to put to sea again.

At noon on Sunday, August 24, we warped out and picked up our breast anchor. Outside the canal entrance buoys we made sail to the sea breeze, southward bound again to rejoin the Humboldt Current on its last lap through Galápagos. After that we would be homeward bound for Tahiti.

The new apprentice was asleep in her basket at the foot of the mainmast.

9. SOUTHBOUND AGAIN— TUMACO

Panama Bay was beautiful as usual. In the evening there was a new moon for a little while. When it had set we looked astern and saw again our familiar trail of wavering phosphorescence. Early in the night we passed San José, one of the Pearl Islands, and set a course across the gulf for Piñas Bay, a sheltered anchorage near the Colombian border.

As we left the islands astern we plunged into a wall of black, lit by incessant lightning and shaken by thunder. The rain came in torrents and lasted until dawn, when it thinned out to reveal the coast looming up deep blue ahead, with the clouds lying heavily on it. We could feel the jump of the current. The breeze had failed us and we approached the land under power.

We planned to follow the coast as far south as the Equator in order to be near ports if anything went wrong. We were not very sure about the mechanics of cruising with a new baby. Before long we realized that Hina was the most contented sailor aboard. In good weather we hauled her basket into a ray of sunlight that streamed down the hatch —and she slept happily. In bad weather we wedged her in beside the mast, and the tireless Pacific rocked her to sleep. Had we known how easy it was we would have made our southing outside of the current. By the time we learned this we were already committed to the coastal route.

We were off Piñas Bay shortly after noon. I was greatly

tempted to take advantage of the calm and get south under power as fast as possible.

"But you said there was a river here," cried Piho accusingly, unbelieving that anyone could possibly pass a place with a river. We were just passing the entrance when Ah You came up to look.

"Ropiti. Just once a river to bathe in before we start across the sea again. It is so long now. Then I can think of that when I am seasick."

Both girls were on the verge of tears.

We anchored in the beautiful, heavily wooded bay. The river was only a small stream, but it cascaded down over a series of lovely falls under a canopy of jungle trees and lacy ferns . . . and just a little way up from the mouth there was a perfect bathing place formed by a low unobtrusive dam that had been built by those hard-boiled *yanquis* from Balboa so they would have a beautiful bathing place on their annual fishing trip to Piñas Bay.

I left the girls there with the washing and went back aboard. Three hours later when I went to get them I found them lying half immersed in the stream, draped over some smooth boulders, with heads downstream and hair flowing in the current—oblivious to the fact that it was evening. Nearby lay a big pile of clothes that they had washed.

Next morning after feeding and bathing Hina the girls disappeared again in the pram with a big pile of washing which I am absolutely sure was the same pile they washed the day before, and which they would wash all over again just for the fun of it.

As we left, at dawn on the third day, our white spars were just beginning to be visible in the first light. It was calm. We crept out under power to begin our bout with the current. As much as possible we would stay very close inshore to avoid it, but often, at the capes and promontories, we would meet it head on.

With fickle breezes alternating with calms, we moved steadily south, sometimes under sail, sometimes power, sometimes both—hugging the steep forested rain coast— past Mono Island and the Colombian border, past frequent tiny round wooded islets close to shore.

Before dark we anchored in Octavia Bay off a crescent beach with a few huts, staying a half-mile offshore for fear of malarial mosquitoes. It was another beautiful anchorage, two miles in behind a mountainous wooded peninsula. Just off the point we caught our supper, this time a fighting five-foot wahoo, half of which we tossed into a family-size sailing *cayuca* heading also into the bay. At night there were the same jungle noises ashore as at Barro Colorado, and the same high-pitched frantically repeated scream we had never been able to identify.

Our nicely planned schedule went to pieces the next day when a fresh head wind prevented us from making Port Utria before dark. This was a disappointment, for Port Utria is a lovely picturesque anchorage. We went on to approach Cape Corrientes by night. This was where the serious part of the voyage began.

Living up to its bad reputation, Cape Corrientes received us with a night of almost incessant lightning, violently breaking current rips, and the general confusion of frequent squalls.

For three nights and two days we endured a succession of the most violent electrical storms imaginable, all from dead ahead. At night they were like incredibly magnified Fourth of July celebrations. A strange pulsating orange-colored lightning alternated with a rare bluish type that progressed across the sky in great arcs, giving off brilliant rocket-like flashes. Several times luminous gaseous globules clung to our mastheads and yardarms for several minutes at a time. Possibly they were a form of the St. Elmo's fire of the ancients. This part of the Colombian coast seems to be afflicted with these remarkable electrical storms, for almost every time I have passed this way it has been the same.

Thus we clawed our way painfully around Cape Corrientes, along the shoal coast past Point Charambirá, and past Buenaventura again, but this time close in to avoid the strength of the current.

The northern coast of Colombia is high, wooded, with deep water offshore and numerous good anchorages. Below Buenaventura it is low mangrove land, much of it flooded from the innumerable rivers, with bars and shoals extending far offshore. In one day we passed a stretch of this coast with fourteen rivers, some of them with deltas that formed several mouths. It is rarely clear enough for the distant mountains to be visible, and all you see are the breakers and the mangroves.

As we progressed south the wind became more and more steady, and harder, always from ahead. During the day, when the wind had a tendency to shift more onshore, we worked as close in as we dared, keeping a constant lookout for floating tree trunks off the river mouths.

As we passed river mouth after river mouth, delta after delta, through discolored water that had us constantly checking the chart and taking soundings, we saw at close hand the origin of the yellow stream of debris that had so vividly bounded our river in the sea on the northbound passage. At night we worked offshore for safety, and to take advantage of a slight shift of the wind, but we never got out into the clear blue of the Humboldt.

On Sunday, the last day of August, we took time out for a few hours of relaxation in the lee of Gorgona Island, which I had passed many times but never before visited. Gorgona is a beautiful wooded high island with a handful of inhabitants. After our botanically minded crew had enjoyed the flowers and trees and a stream, we stocked up on coconuts and headed out again at dusk, for the anchorage was poor.

That night and the next day the head wind was stronger than ever. We inched past the river mouths of Guascama Point, past the shoals of the Rio Patía Delta which were breaking heavily two miles offshore, taking long tacks toward the land until the shoal water forced us about, and short tacks offshore. There were more miles of river mouths and deltas, and green wild coast interspersed with Paumotu-like villages and coconut plantations clinging precariously to the shore trying not to be pushed into the sea by the green jungle behind.

The much-advertised land and sea breezes are apparently nonexistent at this season below Gorgona. The southwest wind blows hard and steadily up the coast, day and night.

We had planned to continue as far as Salinas, at the entrance to the Gulf of Guayaquil, where I had had our mail sent. But we were making such slow progress that we decided to stop at Tumaco instead and have our mail forwarded. From Tumaco we would beat our way into the west-flowing main stream of the Humboldt and follow it to Galápagos and beyond. Late that evening we hove to off the port, with the lighthouse to help us keep position during the night.

✦

Tumaco is the southernmost port of Colombia, the only good harbor between Buenaventura and the Gulf of Guayaquil. It is a depressing wooden settlement of eleven thousand population, with an excellent anchorage formed by three islands. The good but devious entrance channel skirts mangrove-lined shores with rivers and bayous leading off in all directions.

Entering, we passed a big, nearly completed port development on the outer island, with fine docking facilities and a new railroad spur walking out on stilts from Tumaco. The project is supposed to turn this sleepy little malaria- and dysentery-ridden byway into an important seaport to tap the almost entirely undeveloped resources of southern Colombia.

Sailing dugouts with gracefully upswept ends like those in the western Pacific dotted the wide smooth bay. Women stood in the shallows in water up to their waists fishing. Thatch houses here and there along the shore looked vaguely and unexpectedly African. We anchored in a completely landlocked harbor beside the old town.

The boarding party came alongside in a long, outboard-motor-propelled dugout in which everybody stood. They were armed with big .45 automatics in black leather hip holsters. We went into our routine of Napoleon cognac and Tahitian songs by Ah You, and in a few minutes it was Valdivia all over again.

The port captain and customs chief, combined in the person of Captain Fernando Espinosa, sent the dugout ashore with rapid-fire instructions.

"They get my secretary my girl my American friend roommate," he explained. "My girl she sing *bambuco*."

Wondering whether the secretary-girl-American-friend-roommate was one, two, or three persons, and what *bam-*

buco was, we waited while various people tried tentative chords on Ah You's guitar.

Several times the dugout came back loaded, the paddlers out of breath, for the outboard had broken down. The secretary-girl friend turned out to be one person; the American friend-roommate was a young banana trader named Fred Piscani. The girl and several others, including two or three of the revolver bearers, were introduced by the captain as a body.

"Customs department. Very good. You like very much."

Everybody else was anonymous except a tall dignified man named Don Louis Escruceria who was introduced as my *"agente."*

The modest spark of our Tahitian entertainment in Valdivia had set off a first-class night-club act. In little Tumaco it set off a whole musical comedy that was a small-scale Latin-American *Porgy and Bess,* with guitars, wooden drums, gourd rattles, folk dancing and singing in which everyone took part. The heavy-set stern-looking man who handled the rattles wore a .45 which beat a supplementary tattoo on its leather belt. We were delighted with the local custom whereby the girls all sang while dancing with the men. The men joined in for certain songs, and everybody would be dancing and singing at the same time. There was the same utter lack of self-consciousness and affectation as in Tahiti.

Bambuco turned out to be the name of a whole group of songs of the interior, in which the port captain's secretary sang the lead accompanied by some other girls who somehow appeared aboard, plus an unidentified man with a fine tenor voice. The interior of South America must be full of potential talent.

This went on for hours, and ushered in a nine-day stay in

which I learned all about Colombian smuggling, politics, Tumaco history, and the banana-buying business.

One of the few other interesting aspects of Tumaco was the activity on the wide sheltered bay, where beautifully shaped dugouts leaped away from shore like arrows when sail was erected, or surged across the bay to the thrust of standing paddlers who could have been on some remote New Guinea river. When heavy loads were to be carried, balsa logs were lashed alongside to give extra buoyancy. We saw one slender dugout not over twelve inches wide come by with four full-grown steers standing in it.

But although the lively harbor traffic appealed to me, it also caused a certain unrest, for we were in the customary state of siege, more acute than usual because canoes crisscrossed the bay at all hours of day and night. Tino slept forward on deck, Zizi aft, while I took the midships companionway. Occasionally a persistent would-be visitor would drift patiently for the better part of the night within two or three yards of *Varua*, hopeful that everyone aboard would finally go to sleep. Tino would give him cigarettes and pass a word or two with him now and then and the game would go on until dawn.

The nightly siege of hopeful thieves was accompanied by the efforts of hundreds of curious submarine woodpeckers who spent the night tapping industriously on our bottom. All in all the nights were far from dull, and we were grateful for the local custom of sleeping most of the afternoon.

The mail I was waiting for came and we were ready to leave. To repay the kindness of Captain Espinosa and Don Louis and others, we gave a party aboard to which twenty had been invited and over a hundred came. The overflow stayed in dugouts alongside, occasionally changing places with those on board. The party got completely out of our hands from the beginning, turning into an all-night dance with music and entertainment provided by the guests. At dawn our friends left, and when all was quiet except for a solitary guitar player drifting a little way off in a small dugout—perhaps waiting for the market to open—we swept up the debris and got ready to leave.

Don Louis, our *agente*, returned later with our sailing documents, among them a remarkable *Lista de Rancho* which stated that we carried, among many other equally bizarre items, two barrels of salted meat and salt pork, 100 kilos of frijoles, 100 kilos of alimentary paste.

Slightly lightheaded from lack of sleep, we headed out to sea, took a last look at the low mangrove-lined shore, trimmed our sails close, and began our beat into the Galápagos-bound main stream of the Humboldt Current.

There were six days of hard plugging, close-hauled, at a steady angle of heel against the powerful southwest wind, driving, slicing, crunching through the short seas. The bellpull clanged through my sleep more and more frequently to call me on deck for squalls. Sail would be restored as soon as possible afterward to gain all we could before the wind steadied back in its regular quarter. The wind held west of south. Each hour we were farther west and soon, if the wind did not shift, we would have to skip Galápagos and go on to Tahiti without stopping. On the sixth night a fine drizzle blew in with the wind and suddenly, before 9 o'clock, we sailed out from under the overcast into a starlit sky for the first time since leaving the coast.

The wind did not shift, but it did the next best thing and began to slacken. By daybreak it had eased enough so that we could start the engine, steering a straight course for Galápagos.

Nearing the land, the current increased in power, gathering momentum for its last major effort. We could feel the surges and eddies which betrayed the fact that the Humboldt was encountering for the first time islands large enough to dispute its flow. That evening the northern island outposts of the group lay hazily on the horizon ahead.

10. GALÁPAGOS

I had first visited the Galápagos in 1928 and had been enchanted by the out-of-this-world setting. Wild birds had come and perched on my shoulders and I had bathed in little coves with pengiuns, baby seals, and marine iguanas. As I became more familiar with these incredible islands which had been Charles Darwin's natural science laboratory, I became more and more enchanted. In 1934 I had returned to make a film of the wild life. In 1945 again, sailing back to Tahiti aboard *Varua*, I had stopped here and had revisited the scenes of my earlier visits. The war had made little change except for "The Rock," as the army called their island base, which was being closed while I was there. There was also a bust of Charles Darwin in Wreck Bay, erected by the naturalist Victor von Hagen.

In 1945 I had been depressed by the misfortune and tragedy that lay over the places where man had tried to settle, and by the near-extinction of the wonderful natural life in his vicinity—so I resolved this time to avoid the settlements at Wreck Bay and Academy Bay and Villamil, and the hermits of Floreana if any still lived there. This would be an unofficial Galápagos visit. We would touch only the uninhabited parts of the group and see the birds and animals and beasts of the sea, which, after all, are Galápagos to me.

The winds and the current brought us first to lonely Marchena where we were welcomed by the joyous friendly seals, the close-flying boobies, and the distinctive sharp cool scent of Galápagos. We lay there, moving uneasily in the swell, with the sound of the surf a little too close, and the steady low thrum of the trade wind in our ears. The Galápagos Islands have been described as a great cinder pile, which is largely true, although two or three of the islands have fertile green plateaus up in the clouds. Marchena, which rose before us, is utterly desolate, almost completely covered by lava flows.

It was the first time I had visited Marchena and I only stopped because I wanted to see the place where my friend Nuggerud had died in 1934. Nuggerud had been a pioneer fisherman living at Academy Bay. He set out in his little boat, the *Dinamita,* one day for Wreck Bay. With him were a boy and a passenger named Rudolf Lorenz, one of the lovers of the self-styled Baroness of Floreana Island. Although Nuggerud did not know it, Lorenz was attempting to escape from the Galápagos after the murder of the baroness and her other lover, Philippson. The *Dinamita* vanished. Months later the American tuna clipper *Santa Amaro* saw a distress signal on Marchena and found the dehydrated bodies of the two men, beside a frail skiff a few feet back from the beach. Something had happened to the *Dinamita* near Wreck Bay and the cold waters of the Humboldt had carried them inexorably to their last resting place. The remains were still visible with the binoculars, just around a point from the cove where we anchored.

There was a place where the pram could land close by, with red crabs all over the foam-covered lava rocks. Standing there with the heat burning through the soles of my shoes, I tried to think what it must have been like on those scorching clinkers, watching the horizon for the sight of a boat which was never to come—a horizon broken only by Marchena's twin cinder pile, Pinta Island, clearly visible across the strait, and the great volcanoes of Albemarle hazy in the distance.

We had thought of staying there at anchor for the night, but the place was ominous and the Tahitians were terrified by the scene. We left, almost in a hurry.

We then paid a friendly visit to a hidden colony of Galápagos flamingos on a nearby island, one of the few remaining groups of this lovely but persecuted bird. Only a few of us, and the fewer the better, know where the colony is.

We left the pram on the beach while we silently crept through some bushes at the top of the bank, beyond which was a salt pond. There we lay on our stomachs and cautiously peered out at the great rose-colored birds, one of Nature's most beautiful creations. Unfortunately they are endowed with such a delicate nervous system that careless intrusion can send them into a disastrous panic.

The flamingos were completely unaware of our presence, stilt-walking delicately in the shallow water, preening themselves absent-mindedly with their curious hooked bills. When we had seen our fill we crept back the way we had come, gingerly extricated our pram from a family of sea lions who had apparently accepted it as one of them and were cozily snuggled up against it, and went back aboard *Varua*.

There was now a fine trade wind, and for the next day and a brilliantly clear night we sailed purely for sight-seeing purposes. For a few hours we anchored in Sulivan Bay on Bartholomew Island near a great pinnacle rock that protruded from the sea like a monstrous spear. We were within a stone's throw of the beach, which was covered with roaring sea lions who came out in groups through the small surf to patrol around *Varua*, bellowing all the while.

TO THE GREAT SOUTHERN SEA

Later we coasted the shores of grotesque San Salvador which makes one think of an island on the moon with its craters, fumaroles, and lava flows.

As we sailed among the islands it was easy to see how the solid front of the current was being breached as it was diverted one way or another by the great volcanic piles, allowing spearheads of warm equatorial waters to penetrate to its heart, causing remarkable variations in the water temperature. We would swim in a delightfully warm cove and on the opposite side of a point could plunge into icy Humboldt waters. In the whirls and rips where the opposing currents met, great schools of fish hovered, with sea birds overhead. To take advantage of these teeming waters the tuna clippers come all the way from California.

Finally we steered for the five great volcanoes looming through the fine-weather haze in the west where Albemarle lay. For hours we coasted the great lava-covered island with the steady trade wind in our sails. We rounded the northern point by night and headed for Cape Berkeley, which we approached just before dawn, to find an incongruous blaze of lights close inshore. As day broke we exchanged greetings, for it was an old friend, the American tuna clipper *Paramount* from San Diego. We made a rendezvous for that evening in Tagus Cove, and continued on our way.

As the light increased, the familiar outlines of the spectacular coast grew clear. We rounded Cape Berkeley close in, with the exploded crater that forms the cape towering gloomily high overhead like a great gateway. Beneath us the waters heaved and eddied as the Humboldt surged against the jutting promontory.

For the third time in two days we crossed the Equator. A cold southeast wind swept down the bare slopes. We sailed fast in the smooth sheltered waters as Banks Bay opened up before us, illuminated like a stage setting by the sun which was just rising between the two northern volcanoes of Albemarle. Beyond the bay lay the blackened cone of Narborough, the narrow strait, and the familiar headland that marked the entrance to Tagus Cove—international stopping place of all world voyagers.

Narborough obligingly belched forth a mushroom of gray swirling smoke as we entered the strait. A giant ray leaped close by. A sleeping turtle drifted at arm's length. The sea lions dipped and extended their black noses in curiosity. The strait was as smooth as a table and the day full of peace after the night of skirting Albemarle's fanged coast.

We anchored in Tagus Cove just as the plane from the *Paramount* buzzed us and went off toward the south looking for fish. When they found them they would direct the vessel to the spot by radio-telephone. This is the way to fish in the air age.

That evening we were all aboard the *Paramount*, consuming quantities of choice American fruit and ice cream, and watching a movie. These great far-ranging tuna clippers have every conceivable comfort and luxury. Evenings, the men can even telephone their wives and sweethearts in the States.

Most of the men were from our old home port, Gloucester, but had moved to the West Coast to escape the numbing cold of the New England fisherman's life. After two weeks' work in Galápagos they already had one hundred and sixty tons of fish aboard. When they had their load of three hundred and twenty tons they would return to port and share the profits of the trip.

In the morning I climbed to the crater lake and stood on the rim looking down at Tagus Cove, thinking of the small multitude of visitors who had passed this way. There had been the good scientists and the bad; those who took from the precious stock of living things and those like Von Hagen who came to study them in their natural environment. There were the tiny boats in quest of a dream, and great floating palaces escaping from boredom. There was Ralph Stock, who wandered lost among the volcanoes in his *Dream Ship* for days, and Gerbault, who struggled so long against the elements to get here in his motorless *Firecrest*. Before them the buccaneers and the whalers had passed this way, anchored in Tagus Cove, and gone on their way, while Albemarle's five great volcanoes brooded over the island unchanged, and black Narborough across the way belched occasionally.

It was here in Tagus Cove that I had spent the most critical days of my life, with a ruptured appendix, until chance brought the *Santa Cruz* to fish for bait outside the cove and thereby prevent another name from being added to the list of Galápagos tragedies.

I had come to Galápagos in 1934 to make a motion picture with penguins and other wild creatures as actors. In Elizabeth Bay, a few miles down the coast from Tagus Cove, we had erected a complete miniature village, penguin size, around a tiny landlocked lagoon, using lava slabs as building material. We furnished it with penguin-size fixings from the children's department at Macy's in New York.

The sets were complete and we were starting on the picture when the appendix disaster struck. The strange little village was abandoned and unseen by human eye for years. Then one day a scientific expedition chanced to land there. When they returned to California they reported to the newspapers the "mystery" of the lava village, with theories as to how it came to be, the favorite being that shipwrecked

GALÁPAGOS

sailors deranged by suffering and exposure were responsible. All of this was printed quite seriously in the papers, to my unspeakable delight. Now, revisiting these scenes again, I was filled with nostalgia and anticipation.

Tagus Cove introduced Tino and Zizi and the girls to Galápagos fish life, and, for once, gave me a chance to surpass the Tahitians at their own specialty. In Tahiti everyone aboard including little Piho made me look like a rank amateur when it came to fishing lore. Here in Galápagos it was another story. When I suggested that we go in along the shore in the pram and that *I* would show *them* how to fish, they looked at me with lenient eyes, and came along to please me. When we found the sea urchins and the octopus and the crabs just where I had promised, and the fish at exactly the depth I had said they would be, they looked at me with new respect and began to haul them in in a daze.

The next day we were off to Elizabeth Bay, our last stop in Galápagos. We anchored just inside the island I had named Big Penguin Island in 1934. The penguins were still there, and the lovely gray terns, and the pelicans, and all the others. For two days and part of a third I continued in my unprecedented role of tutor to the others in matters concerning Nature, showing them as many of the secrets of Elizabeth Bay as could be revealed in so short a time.

We put the big yawl boat overboard, for the bay would be too rough for the pram, and spent the first morning drifting around the little offshore islands meeting the inhabitants. There was a great bull sea lion living in the nearest rocky cove who took a distinct dislike for Tino and later on chased him into the sea. As we coasted slowly along, rising and falling in the swell just where it started to break over the jagged black rocks with their darting blue and scarlet crabs, the seals came up to look into our faces with big soulful eyes from a distance of two feet. Huge sea turtles did the same thing. The friendly penguins took turns coming to look, calling back and forth all the while in their plaintive owl-like voices.

When the sea breeze came in we rigged the sail on the boat and prepared to cross the bay to visit my old penguin village. Everyone was to go except Zizi, for I try never to leave the ship alone during a voyage. The wind came in fresh from the northwest and the boat pitched noisily alongside *Varua* in the small fast waves, her half-smothered sails slatting madly. It was hard to keep my footing as Hina was passed down in her basket. At the last minute I took pity on Zizi, who looked so forlorn and dejected. At my nod he scrambled over the side and dropped into the boat. I felt better, for participation is one of the things that makes a successful voyage.

"Okay, Tino—cast off."

"Aye aye, Sir, Captain Bligh," replied Tino with a big grin.

Astonished and delighted at Tino's unexpected erudition and sense of humor I shook the sail free, swung the tiller and we leaped away from *Varua* across the wide whitecapped bay.

Because I know Galápagos weather so well I dared to leave the ship alone. It would blow just so hard and from just this direction until sundown. Our big anchor was on good bottom in seven fathoms, with forty-five fathoms of heavy chain out. *Varua* would be all right, but it was a strange feeling to sail away from her with my whole crew, and watch her graceful form grow small.

I had been the first to chart this bay in detail and I knew every shoal and inlet. With a feeling of possession I drove the little boat across the rough bay for over a mile, before the fresh quartering wind. Then we gybed and ran into the sheltered inlet behind Iguana Tree Islet, which I had so named because every day when the tide was too high for the marine iguanas to feed on the sea moss, they would drape themselves all over a large dead mangrove tree there.

My penguin village was still intact. All our old friends, or their descendants, were still there.

We worked our way back through the mangrove islets along the shore, visiting several harems of sleek silky seals who were raising their babies in the sheltered inner passages. Tino and Piho caught lobsters for supper. The sun set behind Narborough and the cold of evening settled down. It was good to get aboard *Varua* and light the stove and drink hot soup while waiting for the booty to cook.

Afterward there was an orgy of fishing far into the night, until our rigging was draped with drying fillets that would be eaten during the voyage. *Varua* moved restlessly in a small swell that found its way in past the two sheltering islets. Both Tino and Piho fell asleep on deck at last, unwilling to give up fishing while there was an ounce of strength left in their bodies, for this was paradise for a Polynesian.

The next day was full to the brim with activity. There was another sailing expedition, this time to the secret inner lagoon where the sea lions go to mate, and where their hoarse bellows were punctuated by the gay song of little vermillion flycatchers that darted over our heads.

When we had explored all the branches of the inner lagoon and visited all the inhabitants, we left them to relax and resume their personal affairs, and wound our way out through the narrow channel. Just outside, where the inlet opens into a branch of the bay, Tino put on his underwater mask and speared more fish to add to our larder.

This time Zizi had remained aboard to complete our salt fish program. When we returned he diffidently showed us the enormous quantity he had caught. We salted the rest of the catch, cleaned up, and relaxed in the peace of the evening.

A few sea lions circled *Varua* once or twice and we could hear the soft night calls of the penguins in the dark water around us. A cool wind came down from the clouds over Albemarle's nearest volcano. The soft night light veiled the grim lava-scorched slopes so that the desolate daytime landscape took on the beauty of any mountain islands seen by night across still waters.

I lay on my back on deck, weary but not sleepy, vaguely hearing the talk of the others as they discussed all the oddities of Galápagos wild life that they had seen. Even Zizi had given up his usual pose of sophistication and had joined the others in their amazement. I thought how this voyage was giving me back something I had had long ago, for through their eyes I was again seeing a strange new world with the childlike wonder and awe that shines through the tales of Homer, Marco Polo, and Ibn Battúta. Not so far from our own time, I thought of the accounts of Magellan's chronicler Pigafetta, Captain Fanning of the American trading ship *Betsey,* and all those other firsthand reports of earlier voyages that had helped draw me into such a life in the first place.

I thought, too, of how we had reached the end of the great ocean highway that had brought creatures of the Antarctic all along the coasts of Chile and Peru, and eventually out to the Galápagos on the Equator itself, where they had slowly adapted themselves to their new surroundings. I thought back to Charles Darwin, who had also followed the Humboldt on the *Beagle,* and who, along its cold path and particularly in Galápagos, had seen what we had seen, and thus conceived his great studies on evolution. We had come to the last stopping place of these creatures of the Antarctic, for beyond lay nothing but wide Pacific Ocean.

When we did fall asleep it was with the knowledge that the next time we turned in for an unbroken night we would be back in home waters.

At dawn the first swimming party of little penguins surrounded the ship and awakened us softly with their plaintive owl-like calls. As we got in our anchor and gathered way, passing very close to the nearest rocky island, the great bull sea lion who lived there stirred himself and plunged in to make sure our intentions were friendly. On the last point was a family of penguins, late risers, too engrossed with their personal affairs to pay the slightest heed to the white brigantine slipping by almost at arm's length. A moment later we were out in the strait.

11. MANGAREVA AND HOME

It was with a great pang that I watched the familiar landmarks grow small astern and fade into the haze at the base of the towering black volcanoes. It was almost surely the last time I would see them.

At 3 P.M. we sailed out from under the land clouds into the sparkling blue Pacific afternoon. We were on our long run now, the always happy passage down the trades from Galápagos to Tahiti. But this time, we were taking a new and unfrequented route: three thousand miles in one jump to Mangareva, down in the southeast corner of Oceania, and from there nine hundred miles to Tahiti.

I had always wanted to visit remote Mangareva. I believed we could sail the longer distance involved more comfortably and probably more quickly than on the usual route via the Marquesas or the Tuamotus, because the prevailing winds would be on our beam rather than astern.

As we coasted along in the smooth water under the lee of Albemarle, Hina was reinstalled at the foot of the mainmast, where she would be safe from the movement of the open sea and where we could keep an eye on her from the wheel. She celebrated our departure by learning to turn over from back to front. For several days she practiced her new accomplishment assiduously, chinning herself to peer over the edge of her basket with big dark eyes, until suddenly she would want to get on her back again but couldn't. So one of the jobs of the helmsman was turning over Hina.

MANGAREVA AND HOME

When we left the shelter of the land Hina braced herself against the roll with one foot on the side of her basket, looking utterly delighted and most abandoned. Later she solved the problem of turning over from front to back, when the ship took a deep roll at just the right moment and she was over before she knew it. For a few days, until she learned to do it all on her own, she timed her turnings with the roll of the ship, and managed quite nicely.

At first after we left Galápagos the breeze was in the south so we used only our fore and aft sails, steering southwest toward the heart of the trades; but gradually the wind shifted, becoming the real southeast trade wind, and conditions were ideal for our brigantine rig. Our daily runs increased. *Varua* began to sing with the steady musical cadence in hull and rigging that goes with passage-making.

The sky was cloudless. *Varua's* colored sails made her an island of sienna red in a blue and white world. More than ever we appreciated the way they reduced the glare. I took to wearing my old sun helmet which made a noise like a peanut vendor's whistle when the wind blew through its vents. When the breeze was light and the sun especially hot, we sometimes used the Japanese paper parasol at the wheel. It was September, and the sun was moving south with us. Since it was directly overhead at midday, these unnautical accessories were a great comfort, although they might give *Varua* a somewhat low rating in conventional yachting circles.

Coming on deck in the soft night to take the wheel, there was again that insidious hypnotic effect of the roll of the ship going with a fair wind. I would study the stars to keep awake, or reach below for the shaded lantern and read a while, curled up in a corner of the well, steering with one hand and the feel of the wind in my ears. Now and then a harsh disembodied cry would come out of the night from an unseen tropic bird overhead. They would be back again by day—usually just a pair of them—to make their swift questioning circles before hurrying off on their always urgent business.

For a while our steering was uncannily affected by vast, slow-turning eddies, and the nights were cold. We knew the Humboldt was still with us. But gradually as the waters merged with the circulation of the Pacific itself to become the Equatorial Current, the chill was absorbed by the vast tropical sea. Suddenly the flying fish were back. I will never forget the first night they began to come aboard. When I relieved Tino at 3 A.M., he already had one beside him. He went forward to turn in, found another, still another, gathering them up sleepily as he went. He began to exclaim "Oh boy!" He came back with his hands full and piled them in a small heap beside the charthouse, and went below.

A little later he reappeared, and to my astonishment picked them all up again and redistributed them in various places all over the ship.

"I care about Piho," he explained. "She come bimeby walk about deck find them."

When he had arranged the last two or three in the most interesting places, so that Piho would have the greatest possible excitement finding them, he smiled to himself and disappeared up forward. From that day on there was a contest between Piho and Ah You to see who would wake up first to make the dawn search. A daily lottery developed as to who would eat them for breakfast, crisp and delicious, if there were not enough to go around.

One evening a whole school of gaily colored squid splattered aboard, spraying everything with ink wherever they hit. It took the better part of the next morning to scrub *Varua* clean again.

For several days we were accompanied by a big school of dolphins. It was their mating season and they were more excited than I have ever seen them before. They would leap through the cresting whitecaps side by side and sometimes shoot ten or twelve feet straight into the air. At night when it was quiet and you lay in your berth, you could hear them through the thin hull planking, talking incessantly back and forth.

One week out, at sunrise on October 1, when we had completed eleven hundred miles of unblemished perfect-weather sailing, we began to have revolving squalls. I had not expected them for another thousand miles. The first one was a sneak squall that crept up unperceived just after I left Piho at the wheel with a clear horizon. Suddenly the gimbal table in the saloon was at an unnatural angle, and you could feel the increased speed. On deck it was blowing hard with fine rain, and shifting to the south. Piho was quite happy and doing the right thing, and Tino was awake and watching her from up forward. It was already easing. Going below again I stopped to speak to Hina at the foot of the mainmast. Her right foot was braced way up on the top edge of the basket against the steep heel of the ship in the squall. She seemed absolutely delighted.

For two or three days the squalls were light. The trade blew faithfully in between. There were sun rainbows by day and moon rainbows by night. Our fragile and patched No. 3 staysail would be hauled down if the squall looked black enough and promptly hauled up again afterward so that the rhythm of our progress never changed. During the few minutes when the squalls were at their maximum, we would alter course as the wind shifted, to keep it on our quarter. I continued to rest well during my night watch below, except that the moon was so bright I kept waking up thinking it was daybreak and I had overslept.

We had fallen into the long-voyage routine by now, with its strange sense of timelessness. The days of the week again became only tiny navigational noon positions marked one by one across the white space of the chart. Suddenly, before we knew it, we were halfway to Mangareva, having made fifteen hundred miles in nine days. We were on the last chart now, with the penciled courses of previous voyages all converging on Tahiti.

I had expected the squalls to be temporary, but as we passed the halfway mark and the afternoon wore on, there were sundogs to windward and a spectacular gold sunset under a perfect arch of towering cloud. After dark, a light shower was followed by the first really heavy wind. There was the familiar Latitude Fifty moan in the rigging for a little while, and surging ten-knot speed.

Ah You was at the wheel this time, calmly following instructions while I stood in the hatchway coaching. Tino and Zizi had the two upper staysails off before they felt the power of the blast, and in two minutes Zizi was back in his galley ready to serve dinner, quite unperturbed. Although the worst squalls always seemed to hit just when Zizi was cooking, he usually had everything so well under control that there was no need for the peculiar hissing expletive that he reserved for moments when something spilled or burned.

From then on the squalls were heavy, interspersed with calms. There was a boisterous confused sea because of the shifting winds in the squalls and because there was no steadying wind between squalls. We lurched and stumbled, sometimes throwing the wind completely out of the sails. We carried more and more sail during the squalls to make up for what we lost between them, for we were using up supplies, and water in particular, with a lavishness that was startling. Never before had I realized how much water a baby required. We were also racing against a diaper shortage, for the endless bales we had stowed in Balboa were disappearing over the side at an alarming rate.

The squalls were thick enough to give one claustrophobia. Most of them were the circular type with clouds reaching close to the sea, but there were none of the waterspouts we had seen under similar conditions on earlier voyages.

On the fifth day of this kind of weather the squalls themselves petered out. Ironically, as we crossed the only five-degree square on our route in which the pilot chart predicted southeast winds of force five we had nothing but light shifting breezes. Then, when we approached the theoretical southern extremity of the southeast trades, the good-weather clouds came drifting across the pale blue sky again and the wind came back to give us one more period of magnificent sailing during which we made the best time of the homeward passage. It was the kind of sailing one dreams about and remembers—surging, lifting, almost flying, with the crests rushing alongside white with foam and the miles reeling by lightly. But overrunning the regular easterly seas there was a heavy southerly swell, reminiscent of our southern passage, and we knew we could not depend on our fine wind to last.

Our wild exhilarating ride was over all too soon, after which, as if to prove that we actually were at the southern limit of the trades, we had two exasperating days of vagrant breezes, showers and calms, through which we obstinately hung on to the two squaresails while they flapped disconsolately or hung like two great window curtains, a far cry from the voluptuous bursting curves they had been. Finally we took them off, just before a wild wet squall one evening which forced most of the rest of the sails off too. But as the wind steadied after the first lashing fury, sail after sail went up and we began to regain some of the miles we had lost.

The new wind settled in the south, as I had suspected it would from the high barometer, and increased hourly. Tomorrow there would be the *maraamu*, the blustering southerly that drives the trading schooners to shelter. But tonight we would use the wind as long as we could.

The discouragement of the doldrum days, when we thought we would have no more wind, flew away with the spume. We had come almost all the way without one of these high barometer southerlies. We had fallen behind the pace I had hoped to maintain to make a record passage, so even the *maraamu* was welcome.

Zizi came up to help with a big smile, despite the fact that he had run out of tobacco and was smoking tea. In the black of night Tino was on the upper crosstrees among the stars hauling away as he stretched the topsail to the yardarms—setting it, not taking it in—and shouting a song about beautiful Tahiti at the top of his lungs for sheer joy as *Varua* felt the added drive of the big squaresails in the increasing wind. Through the tearing surging night we ran off a hundred miles in ten hours.

I thought for the hundredth time what a wonderful ship this was, a spacious seventy-foot hull with lines so perfect that she could make passages that compared with those of the big ocean racers but with a cruising rig that could be handled by two men.

MANGAREVA AND HOME

The *maraamu* lasted only forty-eight hours and was followed on the next to the last day by clear blue skies and trade wind clouds. We were on the last hundred miles to Mangareva. Ah You had recovered from the *maraamu* and was playing Paumotu songs on the guitar to Hina, who now spent most of her increasing waking hours on her elbows, head peering over the top of her basket. Her bright eyes eagerly studied the new world as she began to take an intense interest in everything. She seemed enchanted as she experimented with the various sounds she was beginning to learn. Now and then she would topple over in a heavy sea heave and, making delighted noises all the while, would soon be propped up again on her elbows. She never cried. I began to wonder if the Tahitian custom of spoiling babies was the reason—or should one always take a baby to sea at the age of two months?

Approaching Mangareva we passed close to Minerva, one of those shoals of doubtful position and uncertain existence known as "vigias." Vigias are the bane of navigators, for one is never sure where they are, if they are there at all. According to the Sailing Directions, which neglects to state how she got her name, there seemed no doubt about Minerva's authenticity. A ship named the *Sir George Grey* was assumed lost there in 1865, although the British navy failed to locate the reef a few years later. In 1890 the German bark *Erato* saw the shoal. It was again seen breaking heavily in 1920 ten miles from the position reported by the *Erato*.

To my great disappointment the *maraamu* spoiled our chances of looking for Minerva. For although the wind had gone down to a fresh breeze and we arrived in the vicinity at midday, there was still a big sea running, which broke in an unruly fashion. It was impossible to distinguish breakers caused by a shoal from those left in the wake of the *maraamu*. We steered a course that took us ten miles to the north of the northernmost reported position of the errant shoal, kept a vigilant lookout, but saw nothing.

We had almost reached Mangareva now. The land birds were already with us. Our powerful National receiver picked up the feeble Papeete station. We were also in a peculiar radio area where we caught the bounce-back of the American long-wave broadcasting, and heard hillbilly guitar music on such an incredible number of stations that one would think it was the prevailing form of entertainment in the United States.

Time had passed so quickly that it seemed impossible that the land lay just over the horizon. But we had good sights, and the radio told us that our chronometer time was correct. So that night, when our distance was almost run out, we hove to and lay there keeping a sharp lookout since the reefs are far offshore and there is no lighthouse.

We had run our three thousand miles in eighteen days, averaging about 167 miles a day. This was not sensational but it was much better than we had done on other passages on the more northerly route—and vastly more comfortable because we had escaped the rolling. We still had nine hundred miles to go to Tahiti, making the over-all passage about two hundred miles longer than the shortest route through the Tuamotus. Barring accidents, we should still arrive in less time.

Dawn found us lying five miles off the eastern reef, somewhat closer than we had expected because the ocean drift accelerated as it approached land—another good example of the necessity for eternal vigilance and the danger of depending too much on a taffrail log.

Mangareva is arranged like Bora Bora and Maupiti. It is

MANGAREVA AND HOME

a central high island surrounded by a lovely lagoon and a far-flung reef on which are dotted smaller islands, some of them beautiful high islands in miniature. There are two good passes, one in the west with a fair wind for leaving, and one in the southeastern part which can easily be entered under sail with the prevailing easterly winds.

We ate a leisurely breakfast, waiting until the sun was high enough for us to enter safely and to highlight the unsurpassed beauty of the lagoon. Then we made sail, and with the freshening trade rounded the southern entrance island, Makapu, and sailed in across a sapphire and emerald dream world of fantastic corals, rainbow-hued fish— and an occasional lurking coral head that could disembowel the unwary stranger.

The beacons and buoys were missing, and the entering range for the southern pass did not check. Then, in the narrows at the very entrance to Port Rikitea itself, a dark-colored reef barred the way. I hastily rechecked my position and approached to within a few feet, whereupon the "reef" leaped into action and disappeared: a large school of giant rays that had been sunning themselves there.

Piho and I were at the masthead conning her in, full of joy. Even this remote outpost of Oceania was home to us, for when you live on an island all the islands are your homeland.

In no time at all there were drinking nuts aboard, *tiare tahitis* with their pungent nostalgic perfume on our ears, squawking chickens to eat. But there was no water in the pipe and we would have to get what we needed from the gendarme in tins. We also learned that another yacht had come recently to Mangareva from Galápagos, the *Arthur*

Rogers, and took thirty days. We had already mentioned our eighteen-day run and were quite smug about it.

Somehow the day was gone and we had not been ashore. With the dusk two fishermen glided by in a pirogue, bodies and faces highlighted by their torches. They headed out toward the reef.

We watched the night close down over the island in the evening calm. The last time we had had *tiare tahitis* on our ears was ten months ago, but it seemed like yesterday. And there was Hina now. No one in Tahiti knew about her yet, for we had kept the whole thing as a big surprise. Ah You had been singing to her softly—the song Tino had shouted from the masthead the other night—and now had the sleeping child in her arms. She was telling me that Hina too knew she was coming home.

It was night now, and the lights flickered across the water from the dark island. We recalled the first time Ah You saw the overwhelming blaze of big city lights, in Valparaiso, reaching from the water's edge to the sky itself and as far along the shore as one could see. We counted the lights ashore: five moderately bright ones, seven dim.

"But the torches . . . look at the torches on the reef now. I can't wait to get to Paea."

Every night from our terrace in Paea, we can see the lights on the reef, strung along all the way from Maraa Point to Punaauia. When the flying fish are running it is especially wonderful.

The night land breeze came down from the slopes of Mangareva, carrying out to us a wave of nostalgic fragrance. A cock crowed—the unmistakable Tahitian cock-of-all-hours, with no respect for the time of day or night. We heard a snatch of harmonica and song.

I lay on deck dreamily thinking about it all. These were

the things that attach one to Polynesia, simple intangible unimportant things. Almost affectionately I remembered the other aspects of life in Oceania that had greeted us: the hazardous night approach to an unlit island; the missing buoys and beacons; the bearings that don't check; the water that is not in the pipe. Perhaps there will come a time when I will be more practical and I will wish we had more of American efficiency, and of all those luxuries on which we glutted in the Canal Zone.

I fell asleep there on deck, the solid unbroken sleep one dreams of at sea . . . the ship safely at rest with plenty of chain out, motionless . . . a voyage successfully completed.

Mangareva is a land of the past—a land of ruined still villages of stone and coral blocks; of incongruous ruined ecclesiastical buildings—and it is a land of a ruined race. The ruins, and the cathedral which stands today, are the monument to the mad priest Laval, who became obsessed with his dream of creating on this remote Polynesian island a great religious center . . . and in so trying, destroyed not only an ancient culture but the population as well.

It was in the year 1834 that Honoré Laval of the Jesuit order of Picpus arrived in Mangareva, accompanied by a brother priest who lacked Laval's ambition but was to prove invaluable because he had studied architecture. Narrowly escaping death at the hands of the Mangarevans, they were able in a short time to convert the king, Maputeoa, who was soon a tool in the hands of Laval. The priest became, in fact, absolute ruler of the islands, destroyed the old gods, drew up new laws to suit his purposes, and ruled with an iron hand.

With his power established, Laval began his vast building projects. It is said that Laval had the entire able-bodied population outside of essential food gatherers working under a system of forced labor like the ancient slaves of Egypt who labored under the Pharaohs on the pyramids. Those who lacked enthusiasm, or who sinned and were caught, were thrown in the windowless dungeons that still stand today because they were built like great beehives, all in stone.

Two large towns were built, of stone and coral. Wherever there had been a native shrine Laval built a church. In the two towns, Rikitea and Akamaru, he built cathedrals bigger than the one in Papeete. He built a great convent on the hill overlooking Rikitea and incarcerated the passionate Polynesian girls there behind a massive wall of coral blocks. Elsewhere there was a monastery and an ecclesiastical college. There were triumphal archways and great stone stairways up the hill. There seemed no end to the projects, all massively executed in great coral blocks cut out of the reef in the burning sun.

Laval's dream had taken solid form. But so many people had died that the great buildings were empty and there were fewer and fewer to attend mass in the imposing churches.

The French governor who finally came from Papeete to investigate the strange tales filtering out of Mangareva is said to have confronted Laval with the birth and death records, which showed that five thousand men and boys—over half the population—had died in ten years from the effects of the forced labor. Laval is said to have replied: "It is true they are dead. But they have gone to Heaven that much more quickly."

Laval was eventually removed, but it was too late. Mangareva never recovered. What was left of the population had lost the spark that keeps a people alive. Today there are about fifty Mangarevans left, in four or five families which can no longer intermarry. There had been nine thousand when Laval arrived.

Man has always destroyed man, and probably always will, for ideals, for greed, or for the simple urge to dominate—but the saddest thing is when religion, determined to save a race, brings about its destruction.

Today all is ruin in Mangareva. The towns Laval built are empty and overgrown. The great convent with its mile-long wall, the college over on another island, the other buildings that are lost behind the tropical jungle . . . all are ruins. We walked among the great piles of stone, many of the walls still standing today, with full-grown trees crowding each other inside the halls. Only the churches stand undamaged, maintained by the handful of the faithful who still live . . . and the magnificent eight-hole stone privies that had been built for the nuns.

One other thing also is left. Laval somehow found time to make a painstaking compilation of Mangarevan records and customs, which remains a unique document about ancient Polynesian life. Thus the man whose obsession sealed the doom of the Mangarevans ironically provided the finest record we have of that race.

On the hill behind Rikitea stands the monument to the last king of Mangareva, Maputeoa, whose power melted before the hypnotic force of the mad priest. It is a jewel-like stone chapel of beautiful proportions. Inside lies the king's tomb, with his obituary scratched roughly on a corroded sheet of copper. It is open to the weather. The red tiles of the roof were taken by the mission to repair a church building in the village. Recently the beautiful supporting columns of the little chapel were torn out and reinstalled at they would open and release their stored-up perfume and be made into *couronnes* to be worn on the head. I had promised that we would find the ferns and leaves somewhere on the way.

As we passed the little green *motus,* one after the other, she would look at me, questioning, "This one?" And I would tell her, "No, not this one; we are still too far from Tahiti."

Then one day I said, "This one," and we went ashore in the pram to look for ferns and certain leaves with which to weave the *couronnes*—Hina as pert as a mina bird in her basket, Ah You, and Piho, and I. We sat on the dazzling white beach of the uninhabited island in mid-Pacific weaving wreaths to wear on our heads when we got back to Tahiti. Hina looked on calmly and intently with her big dark eyes. It was all the same to her—Samba dancing in Colombia, lurching through bad squalls, sailing down the trades, or weaving wreaths on a deserted mid-ocean atoll. We wondered what language she would speak, poor Mea, as we talked to her in three.

We sailed on, with a dying wind, cleaning, polishing, and painting so that the ship would gleam from stem to stern for homecoming. Hina in her basket was moved around like a Balinese fighting cock so that she could watch.

Finally, there were no more islands and no more wind. With three hundred miles to go, we went on under power. There was not a breath from any direction, not a squall. Even the swell was gone. So at the very end we experienced that rarest of conditions, a dead calm with a motionless sea in trade wind latitudes. At night the sea was incredibly beautiful, with a surface of polished onyx disturbed only by the silver ripples of our wake.

The voyage was almost at an end now. Peace lay over

the ship. Ah You strummed softly on the guitar for Hina in her basket at the foot of the companionway. My eyes moved from compass to them, and back, as I waited for Tino to relieve me. Up forward, Zizi was visible in the galley hatchway as a spot of fire, as he drew on his cigarette, waiting for supper to cook.

It had been a happy voyage, thanks to the dignity, tact, and indestructible good humor of the Tahitians. There had been harmony, and the same crew throughout the voyage. I thought of Mulhauser, Conor O'Brien, and so many others with their constantly changing crews, and of the countless voyages that break up in Tahiti after one long stretch at sea. The question of compatibility is the skeleton in the closet of ocean cruising.

I suppose Tino and Zizi had sworn a hundred times like myself, when things were bad, never to go to sea again. But they would remember only the trade wind days, the landfalls at dawn, the strange ports. Zizi had broken his knee on *Varua* while clowning one day on a Honolulu voyage, and scalded his foot another time when the ship heaved at the wrong moment. He had spent endless weeks cooking in a hot heaving galley—and he was aboard with his bundle under his arm an hour after I asked him if he wanted to make the southern voyage. Tino had suffered the cold on big schooners to Vancouver in the old days. Zizi knew of the cold only at second hand, his previous limit having been Rapa in the south, Honolulu in the north. Neither gave it a thought.

It had been interesting to watch the two men during the voyage. Tino was still the unchanged enthusiastic child of nature. The success of his nondrinking resolution had allowed him to save his money so that he brought home clothes, materials, and dresses for his family, along with his great moral superiority over the fallen Zizi. Zizi himself, the man of the world, brought back only one new hat (for himself), a pipe which he could not smoke, and vast sophistication.

Another day dawned and the amazing calm was still unbroken. There was nothing but the glasslike sea, the sun, and distant clouds just barely visible above the horizon. Piho insisted she could see Tahiti two hundred miles away. In all my years at sea I had never seen it so calm. It was also so hot that we had to stop painting because the paint blistered. It was practically finished in any case, and *Varua*, ten years old now, looked as if she had just come off the ways.

As we throbbed our way across the calm we rigged a better awning, large enough to shelter all of us from the really scorching sun. Under it we weighed the various approaches to Tahiti. Should we skirt the famous Pari, and Teahupoo, and cut across to the Paea coast where we could see our house and make sure that all was well with the trees and the mountain, or should we come around the other side of the island past Point Venus and in the Taunoa Pass, to salute our friends the Hirshons, who live there, and surprise Port Captain Bailly by entering Papeete harbor from around Fareute Point, unseen until the last minute?

There was another night, our last at sea. The engine throbbed quietly on, unobtrusively pushing *Varua* along at her steady six knots. The mirror of black onyx still lay unbroken except for the wavering silver trail astern. But the night had a weird quality. In spite of the cloudless sky there was an unreal misty something that lay over us like a veil, and we felt as if *Varua* were floating in infinity.

We lay on deck, excited, sleepless, and talked of what

we had seen and done. I tried to find out what the others thought about the various places, but the Tahitian is very diffident about expressing his intimate thoughts and it is only by an unsolicited exclamation now and then that you have an indication.

It had been a strange and unreal voyage in many ways. As we lay on our backs watching the masthead, shining white, pointing strangely still at a starry sky infinitely far away, we kept thinking back to Valdivia and our river existence there. We talked again of the people who were so kind: Captain Froese first of all, and Señora Rudloff; the group who came one day from a ranch far inland expressly to visit *Varua* and bring presents; the severely chic cowboys, especially the one who came all alone one day in a hired *bote*, very tall, very handsome, very embarrassed; and Rosita, who would come and eat grapes with Piho up on the foreyard.

But could they live in Valdivia, I asked.

"Aué, no! The cold," they exclaimed.

"But Panama," Ah You went on, speaking for the others, "the flowers, the beautiful trees and everything green . . . the rain, and the breeze every day from Taboga . . . hot enough but not too much . . . and the ships going by— there perhaps we could live."

"And Cape Horn?" I prompted her. "What about Cape Horn?"

"Tahiti was a dream then. I never thought to see Tahiti again," she said. "I will never, never forget Cape Horn."

It is hard to imagine what she went through those days down south, seasick almost constantly, and cold, but, curiously, never frightened. Until this voyage I had never really understood how much she loved Tahiti and especially our home at Paea. I remembered what she had said in Balboa as we were about to sail:

"It has been wonderful . . . Cape Horn . . . Chile . . . snow on the Andes . . . Panama. But the greatest pleasure is the valley at Ofaipapa and the flowers—and I would like to pull some weeds in the lawn."

Tino remembered the river in the sea with its teeming life and plunging clouds of birds, and most of all Galápagos, where the fish bite until your arms are weary, and where the great sea lion who chases intruders lives.

None of them mentioned the things man has done, the fantastic bridges and tunnels in the Andes, the million-dollar luxury hotels, the great locks of the Panama Canal—not even the glittering cinema palaces of Panama. It is nature they loved and remembered, even little inconsequential incidents, such as a row of pelicans sitting like little old men on the pier at Callao watching the boats go by. These were the things that were in tune with themselves and that reminded them of their beloved island, which they had come to love even more than ever as a result of the voyage.

Again I thought of the spontaneous exclamation of one of the girls one day in Valparaiso when I asked them what they would like to do:

"But there is nothing to do here . . . unless, perhaps, we might go ashore and eat some Chile raw fish."

The greatest thrill of the voyage for them was the return to Tahiti. I wondered if for all of us it was the same, not necessarily just the returning, but the returning after a successful voyage. All the same, I knew that as time passed the things they had seen and done would assume greater and more fantastic proportions, and that the tales they would tell would be repeated and adorned until they would rival the experiences of Marco Polo himself. There might even come a day when they would be saying, "I am thinking of Panama (or Lima, or Valdivia)—there is so much to do there."

Was the voyage a success? We hadn't discovered anything, unless that was really a shoal we saw down in 48° S. We had made only the bare acquaintance of the "westerlies" in the very latitudes where Maury had written that the ship would "find herself followed for weeks at a time by these magnificent rolling swells, driven and lashed by the 'Brave west winds' furiously." For only a day or so had we felt "the great wind roaring fresh behind us and the seas breaking high." Perhaps the satisfaction I felt as we neared home was that of having accomplished what we set out to do, under even more difficult circumstances than I had expected, and of having become a member, junior class, of the brotherhood of navigators who sailed those waters.

I knew that our return was going to be one of the great emotional peaks of a lifetime and that I would attach myself with all my energy to my valley and stream at Paea and my island of Taiaro like a returning lover. *Varua* would probably lie waiting a long time before she again felt the heave of the open sea. But already I had forgotten the head winds, the cold gale nights, and there was a sadness. I would miss the delightful creeping warmth of the new day after the penetrating chill of the dawn watch. I would miss the pulsing, flaming night wake and the glitter of the sea by day and the voluptuous aloneness out there. I knew deep down that sooner than I could now believe I would be longing again for the sea, for its beauty and its cruelty and its often tormentingly ceaseless motion.

For a long time I lay there after the others had turned in.

Strange disconnected thoughts kept running through my mind. The rhythmic throbbing of the engine through the long calm had made me think of those other-life train voyages of childhood because it sounded like the rhythmic pound of the rails that had left such enduring nostalgia. Fearful that the rhythm might be broken while the calm still lasted I went down and hovered over the beautiful engine—and who was to say that a ten-year-old diesel that has run whenever called upon, through all climates and all conditions of fuel and water, is not beautiful—as if my hovering would help see it through. I thought how marvelous it was that a tank full of oil out of the earth could be trickled slowly through some metal parts and thus propel us across the miles of what would otherwise have been deadeningly tiresome calm. Like the engineer on the *Trinidad* who at fifteen-minute intervals stood off six feet and heaved water on his engine, I would not vary my oiling and greasing ritual every two hours for anything.

I stood my last dawn watch. Later, in the after-dawn clarity, Tahiti lay on the horizon ahead, sharply outlined as if cut out of black cardboard. Afterward I gave the wheel to Piho and slept a while. When I awoke I lay there luxuriously for a time listening to the steady throb of the engine and looking out the porthole by my pillow—a porthole that surprisingly was not sweeping arcs across the sky but which gazed steadily out over a shimmering blue-glass sea with white puff clouds overhead. All clear and motionless on the otherwise level horizon stood the truncated cone of Mehetia, the landmark on the approach to Tahiti.

All that morning there was the same broiling breathless calm, lovely to behold, and not too bad to support when one thought where we had been. Tahiti was veiled in the heat haze. At noon, with seventy miles still to go to Papeete, I moved back the clock for the last time, to Tahiti time. We had decided to approach by the Pari, Teahupoo, and Paea. Still the calm held, and still we throbbed our way through it.

At sunset we were about eighteen miles from Presqu'ile, the southeast peninsula of Tahiti. The clouds hung motionlessly over the peaked mountains, reflecting and shimmering in the glassy sea. The heat receded slowly as night came on. There was silence aboard as we coasted along off Teahupoo, the moonlight casting silver reflections on the breaking reef. At last the land exhaled, as the cool air flowed seaward with its perfume of *fara* and wild *pua* and ylang-ylang.

"Tahiti," sighed Tino, half aloud, half to himself. "Ten months." He was echoed by the others, who repeated the word as if it were a magic sesame.

"No more humis," remarked Ah You, irrelevantly thinking of sea lions; while Piho who had just come down from spending the day on the topsail yard suddenly groaned, and offered a little devotional of her own.

"Panama . . . 'Melican escrime . . . ah-ah-ah."

"Valdivia," said Zizi, not to be left out, thinking of the brewery there.

Presqu'ile was fading gradually into the moon haze as we started to cross the bay, beyond which lay our own part of the island . . . the coast of Papara, Paea, Punaauia.

"Valparaiso was as big as all Presqu'ile," observed Piho, suddenly. "It's funny, Tahiti seems much smaller now than it was . . ."

At eleven o'clock I stopped the engine and we heard Tahiti—the rumble of the Vairao reef—distant, familiar.

TO THE GREAT SOUTHERN SEA

The land breeze was just enough to give steerageway as we ghosted along, heading toward Maraa Point and home.

As the sun rose we were off Atimaono, almost home. The pale green of the sugar cane was in sharp contrast to the rest of the coast. The breeze had vanished again and we lay motionless, and very happy, unwilling to hasten the end of the voyage. We spoke to the tuna fishermen in their little outrigger canoes a mile outside the reef. They were intent on their fishing and conversed matter-of-factly as if they had not noticed that we had been away, we who had been down in 50° South.

Tino and Piho shouted with excitement as familiar landmarks were picked up. Later we were quiet and already sad at the impending traitorous desertion of *Varua*. Only Tino would stay, to care for her and keep her ready.

The faint morning breeze we had been waiting for came in and we started to move again, coasting silently along the Paea reef. In there, barely visible behind the ironwoods, we saw the brown thatch of our pandanus roof, and, higher up, the trees we had planted on the upper plateau to protect our valley's rainshed. We entered by the back door, the little crooked pass at Taapuna. The coconut radio had functioned from the other end of the island where we had been sighted, and our two best friends were waiting there in a motorboat to accompany us the last mile or so. At our home mooring in Papeete we sat on deck, happy and sad, not wanting to move for a while as we breathed the old Papeete smell of dust, copra, and sunshine mingled with the perfume of our wreaths of *tiare tahiti* from Mangareva and ferns from the mid-ocean atoll.

APPENDICES FOR THE PRACTICAL SAILOR

APPENDIX 1—VARUA

The name *Varua* is Tahitian for the spirit, or soul.
Varua's registered U.S. Customs dimensions are as follows:

Length	66.2 ft.	
Breadth	16.2 "	
Depth	6.6 "	
Net Tonnage	37	tons
Gross Tonnage	43	"

Other vital statistics: Overall length, 70 ft. Waterline length, 60 ft. Total sail area, 2,700 sq. ft. Sail area, fore and aft sails only, 1,900 sq. ft. Lead ballast on keel, 30,000 lbs. With tanks one-third full and average supplies aboard she draws 7½ ft. and displaces 50 tons. With tanks full and stores aboard for a long voyage she draws just under 8 ft. Water tanks, 625 gallons. Diesel fuel, 800 gallons. A.B.S. rating is * A 1 Y S.

CONCEPTION—DESIGN—CONSTRUCTION

Everyone who has voyaged in small craft has a dream ship, which I expect, like mine, takes varying forms with the years. I have had experience with both fore and aft, and square-rigged craft, having built them as well as sailed them. My dream ship accordingly passed through various phases, but eventually reached a stage of perfection beyond which I could think of nothing to change. Early in 1940 I decided to go ahead with the final design and construction plans.

I had already drawn detailed plans of what I considered the ideal arrangement for my purposes, an approximate profile and deck plan, and a sail plan of a highly specialized brigantine rig. I had made sketches of the general hull form that would be required for a small, fast ship that could go anywhere safely. I knew the fallacy of massive wooden construction, falsely assumed to represent great strength, and was anxious to perfect a radical new type of what is called composite construction, steel and wood combined. I planned to build the ship in my own yard in Ipswich, Massachusetts, and hoped to use the same type of construction later, if successful, for our commercial work.

Thus I had all the preliminary plans and data, but I was not deceived into thinking I was technically qualified to develop the final lines and construction plans. I had seen the unhappy results of building to amateur or incompetent plans and was determined to have the best available technical skill go into the ship.

There were several men who could have developed an excellent final design for me, but one in particular seemed to have everything I wanted. Starling Burgess was best known for having designed the *Ranger*, last, and possibly greatest, of the America's Cup defenders. But he had also designed outstandingly successful ocean racers with cruising comfort and beauty as well as speed. He was the designer of the famous *Niña*, and the great racing fishermen *Mayflower, Columbia*, and *Puritan*. Almost equally important, Burgess also was intrigued with the possibilities of composite construction.

We entered into an arrangement whereby he was to work out the final design around my preliminary plans and ideas, collaborate with us on the development of the composite construction, and consult on related technical problems during building. Burgess was to design a hull just large enough to contain my arrangement plan, whose draft was not to exceed eight feet with tanks full and all stores aboard. The hull was to conform to my unique sail plan and was to be strikingly beautiful, for the esthetic character of a ship is as important to me as its practical qualities. Fortunately Burgess's ideas of beauty coincided exactly with mine.

A beautiful hull was designed which we tank tested at Stevens Institute, devising special techniques for the purpose, since previous tests had been concerned mostly with fine windward work. I was more concerned with fast safe reaching and running, maximum security from broaching to in a following sea, minimum pitching, and easy motion in general. Our model was pared off here and filled out there and refined in every way until the best compromise around the desired characteristics was reached.

APPENDICES FOR THE PRACTICAL SAILOR

I was rather startled to find that it took a hull of fifty tons displacement, sixty feet on the waterline, and seventy feet overall, to contain my arrangement and still achieve the required performance characteristics. A seventy-foot brigantine seemed pretty big to be handled by two men, which was a major requirement, but when we adapted my sail plan to the final hull we found that we could still keep the area of the largest sail within the five-hundred-square-foot limit I had set, which meant that it could be done.

As we developed the construction plans we felt like pioneers. Composite construction was being widely used in Europe but had a bad name in America because of faultily executed early efforts. Bearing in mind the pitfalls to be avoided, mainly electrolysis, we developed a type of construction in which we had complete confidence, and which would be simple to build. The entire structural skeleton of the ship was steel, with wooden planking and decking. Marine plywood was extensively used in the interior. The design gave the advantages of steel, strength with lightness, and almost 20 per cent more usable space inside the hull than the conventional wooden vessel, but avoided characteristics I did not like in all-steel construction. The American Bureau of Shipping approved the plans. Later, the *Varua*-type construction served as prototype for mine sweepers we built for the navy.

In the winter of 1940-41 work was slack at the shipyard in Ipswich. We had just launched two draggers and had only one vessel under construction. A place was prepared off in a corner of the yard where she would not interfere with our commercial work, and *Varua*'s keel was laid. She took a long time to build because we were experimenting with the most efficient ways of handling the new type of construction, and because men were put on her only when it did not interfere with the other work. She took shape slowly but steadily and was launched March 19, 1942.

Starling Burgess was swamped with other work by then so I asked my friend L. Francis Herreshoff to give us the benefit of his wide experience in designing the details of spars and rigging. His beautiful *Ticonderoga* (ex-*Tioga*) and *Landfall* are in about the same class as *Varua*. I have always been proud that these two splendid designers both had so much to do with the development of *Varua*. American yachting suffered an irreplaceable loss in the death of Starling Burgess not long afterward.

Varua has proved ideal in every respect for my special purposes. Although under-rigged in comparison with ocean racers she makes consistently good and sometimes record passages, with a crew of only one or two men besides myself. After long experience with it I can think of no improvements to the rig. Her motion and handling leave nothing to be desired. Similarly, with the hull itself, there are only two or three things I would change. I wish she were coppered, something that could not be done when she was built because of priorities. Another time I would omit the tumble-home of the cabin-house sides so that cabin windows would not drip inside if left open in light rain or spray. One other feature was corrected after the first voyage: a six-inch armored guardrail we ran around the ship, which protected *Varua* magnificently from careless pilot boats and bumboats, but which pounded in a beam sea in spite of its wide V section. We took it all off after arriving in Tahiti, except the parts that served as rigging channels, which are not long enough to cause trouble.

The hull is as strong as the day it was launched, and has proved itself under all possible conditions. The arrangement is ideal for my particular requirements. If I were to do it all over again today, and had unlimited funds to work with, I would reproduce *Varua* exactly as she is, which is saying a great deal after thirteen years of trial.

SAILS AND SAIL PLAN

The sail plan and photographs will help explain *Varua*'s easy handling. Many years of study and experiment went into this rig. It was developed to be effective in the variables as well as in the trades or westerlies, and had to be easily handled on long voyages by no more than two men. It is actually two rigs in one, for when the squaresails which make it a brigantine for fair-wind passages are furled, it becomes a moderately canvased staysail schooner for windward work. Its nearest counterpart in appearance is perhaps the Mediterranean polacca brigantine. Its adaptability to ocean crossings both with and against the wind makes one think of the cod fishermen of Paimpol, Brittany, who evolved a somewhat similar rig for their voyages to and from Iceland, but with a gaff sail between the masts instead of staysails.

APPENDICES FOR THE PRACTICAL SAILOR

The plan offers numerous sail combinations for various conditions. The mainsail is the only sail with a reef but is hardly ever reefed because of its moderate area. Sail reduction is accomplished instead by taking off one or more of the staysails or one of the squaresails. The freedom from gaffs is a blessing, and the only boom on the ship is always under perfect control with its lifts and permanent boom guys. A system of blockless, silent sheets for fore and main staysails contributes to *Varua*'s clear decks and paucity of gear. The sheet simply splices to the outer of a pair of oversize clew cringles, passes around the overhead pipe traveler and back through the second cringle, the whole giving the effect of a double block with becket, and a single block. Upper staysails and fore course sheet to the bulwarks. The mainsheet leads to a beam across the stern davits over the taffrail, and jibsheets lead through blocks on the catheads. Without sheets to trip over, or blocks to stub toes against, the deck is clear from bow to stern.

The reader will have an idea of how we handle sail from the text. It is surprising how fast fore and aft sails, particularly staysails and jibs, come off with proper downhauls, which are usually neglected on yachts. On the two upper staysails the downhauls are combined with brails so that by hauling on one line the sail is brought down and smothered at the same time.

Squaresails on yachts are usually makeshift devices, poorly rigged, and too narrow and deep. Ours are fully accredited members of the rig, proportioned as squaresails should be. All manner of complicated arrangements have been tried to lead squaresail gear down to the deck. I prefer the simpler device of mast ladders to get a man safely up to the yards, and there to have an adequate aperture through the top structure to hold him safely in place while working. A single endless line to each yardarm hauls the squaresails out on track like big window curtains, and brails them in to the mast for furling. As the man descends the mast he passes lashings (which are always there) through the ladder rungs and around the brailed-in sail which molds itself neatly against the fore side of the mast. The foresail yard is at a fixed height, swinging on a simple and effective crane I designed for the purpose, and which can be seen in the photograph. The topsail yard lowers when not in use into fixed slings, to a position just above the lower yard. It has simple smothering lines operated by the weight of the yard as it is lowered, that gather up the bulk of the sail by the time the yard is down. It is then brailed in like the other one, and formed into a neat bundle on the little platform of the top. The foremast, which has to carry the extra strain of the square yards, is a solid, built-up spar, stronger than a natural-grown stick would be. The mainmast is of conventional hollow box-type construction, with extra heavy sections.

We make it a practice when handling sails to run downwind. If you are sailing 8 knots in a 40-knot wind and run up into it to handle a sail as is usually done, that sail will have to face an effective wind of 48 knots at the moment when it is most vulnerable. By running downwind under the same conditions you not only reduce the effective wind force to 32 knots, but you blanket the forward sails in addition. For the same reason, as well as to avoid the strains of pitching into a head sea, we usually get the ship on the other tack by a controlled gybe, rather than coming about into the wind. These tactics contribute greatly to crew safety, and sails that avoid the flogging received when coming about last far longer.

Another point which might be mentioned in passing is the frequently misapplied small-boat axiom of letting her come up into it for squalls. We always run *down* wind, again to benefit from the very important reduction in apparent wind, as well as to avoid flogging sails. Rarely is a properly set sail damaged when running. They are usually lost when allowed to shake under strain.

As to the sails themselves, we have not tried any of the new materials. Weights and type of canvas used are indicated opposite the sail plan. The sails are colored a terra-cotta red which is picturesque and gives complete relief from the glare of white sails. Anyone who has once cruised with dark sails is not likely to go back to white. When I color my sails I treat them at the same time with a mildew-proof water-repellent solution. One treatment will last the life of the sails. Originally I prepared the solution by adding a quart of painter's burnt sienna ground in oil to each gallon of a preservative called Ceraseal. This is no longer available, but most canvas preservatives are based on zinc naphthenate which comes in a concentrate of about 8-10 per cent zinc and must be reduced to about 2½ per cent with mineral spirits before use. Recently I have used this, adding color as before, one quart to each gallon. Spontaneous combustion may occur if the sails are not absolutely dry before being put away after treatment. To be safe, they should be left spread out in the open air for several days. Treating and coloring sails yourself is an economy, although quite a job. Results are satisfactory, although the color is apt to be uneven, like the Breton fisherman's tanned sails.

Recently, having heard a lot about Barfair, I corresponded with the manufacturer about mixing it with burnt sienna to get my favorite color, but they advised against it, recommending that sails be sent to them for treatment and coloring. This being impractical from Tahiti, where we usually make our own sails, I have tried an experiment recently, treating a new mainsail with Barfair, and then giving it a coloring treatment afterward consisting of burnt sienna in a carrier of four ounces of boiled linseed oil to each gallon of kerosene. It remains to be seen how it compares with my old treatment.

AUXILIARY POWER

Sentimentality about sailing without an engine may be left to a few diehards. The question today is what form the auxiliary power should take. This involves two basic decisions. The first, gasoline versus diesel, has only one answer as far as I am concerned: diesel, for its greater safety if for nothing else. The second question, whether it should be high, medium, or low speed, is not so easily answered. My requirements call for the latter, regardless of extra weight and size. No engine has yet been built that is as dependable as a heavy-duty, two-cycle, slow-speed diesel. Mechanics in the most remote ports can understand it, which is not always true of the modern high-speed diesel. There is so little to get out of order that they will run practically forever if you are meticulous about giving them clean fuel, oil, and water. The higher initial cost is saved many times over by economy of operation. Cruising radius is vastly greater for a given tank capacity than with any other type. The sound of these engines is comforting compared with the whine of their high-speed cousins.

The extent to which I am going against today's trend is indicated by the fact that I had to buy a foreign engine. America builds splendid heavy-duty diesels in larger sizes, but Europe has had more experience in the low horsepower range. *Varua* has a German Deutz diesel, two cylinder, two cycle, 47 h.p. at 600 r.p.m. It is air starting, and turns a 30" diameter by 18" pitch two-blade Hyde feathering propeller which offers very little drag when sailing. It is off center, where a small wheel is most effective. This also avoids cutting a propeller aperture, with its attendant drawbacks. As the engine rotation is clockwise (facing forward), the propeller is on the port side where the torque counteracts the slight off-center thrust.

Forty-seven h.p. is obviously not enough for strong head winds or a rough sea. It gives us better than seven knots in smooth water, enough to get us across calm belts or in and out of port, which is what it is for. When sailing closehauled in light breezes we sometimes use it to gain speed and point closer to the wind. This can be useful at times. It is comforting, and good insurance, to have a dependable auxiliary aboard a sailing vessel.

ELECTRICAL EQUIPMENT

While building draggers for the Gloucester fishing fleet I became familiar with the Lister, which was almost universally used on these vessels to drive the electrical plant. This is an English heavy-duty diesel, remarkably dependable and economical. We chose the single-cylinder, 5 h.p. model, turning 500 r.p.m. It is connected to a Diehl 1.5 kw generator which charges a bank of 250-ampere-hour 32-volt Surrette marine batteries. A Janette rotary converter of 300-watt capacity changes the current to 110-volt AC so that low-consumption fluorescent lighting, standard photographic enlarging equipment, and standard radio equipment can be used. Navigation lights, the stove blower, and a Groco electric toilet operate directly from the batteries on 32-volt DC.

Normally, when living aboard, we run the Lister twice a week for about five or six hours to charge the batteries. The rest of the time there is nothing to disturb the peace, for the converter is noiseless.

For years I believed electricity aboard a yacht was more trouble than it was worth, as well as being undependable. When I broke down and decided that *Varua* would have it, it was installed according to best marine practice. In thirteen years the system has never failed.

APPENDICES FOR THE PRACTICAL SAILOR

I have not come all the way yet. We still use hand pumps for fuel, water, and bilge. The forecastle toilet and the one off the engine room are hand models. The most important holdout is electric refrigeration. We still have an icebox. To have electric refrigeration would mean running the generator several hours a day, which I have so far been unable to accept.

ENGINE ROOM

Here is where most designs bog down completely. I have never seen anything so impractical as 99 per cent of the mechanical installations on cruising yachts, and just about that percentage seem to have constant trouble. If you are going to have auxiliary power and electricity aboard, you want it to work. In order for the equipment to stay in condition it needs to be kept clean, dry, and well ventilated, with plenty of space around it. You cannot take care of mechanical equipment if you have to crawl around on your knees to get at it. I know, because I am my own engineer.

I make it a religion to check everything once a week, clean it and oil it and give it a short maintenance run to circulate the oil. It is a pleasure because I can walk around everything in an erect position and everything is easy to get at. The room is so clean and well ventilated that there is no smell whatever. I shudder when I think of the installations I have seen, even on ships twice as big, and the tricks and devices to hide the engine on smaller craft.

I would sacrifice my saloon to have a good engine room if necessary. We actually added several feet to *Varua* so that ours would be adequate. It is nine feet long and the full width of the hull. If your ship is too small to do this sort of thing why not be frank about it and put your engine right out in the open somewhere with a nice safety fence around it. Keep it polished and admire it. It will reciprocate and run for you when you want it.

SAFETY FEATURES

To combat what is to me the greatest single hazard in ocean voyaging —losing someone overboard—*Varua* is so fenced in at sea with three-foot-high double lifelines all around plus boat booms lashed waist high between fore and main rigging, that it would be quite a feat to fall overboard. The bowsprit is ten inches wide, flat on top, with double footropes backed up by bow nettings.

Attached to the framework of the stern davits, within reach of the helmsman, are two life rings, each with attached automatic waterlights. I hope we never have occasion to use them, but if we do, they are there.

After "man overboard" comes "fire" in the list of hazards at sea. If your house catches fire you can call the fire department. I can think of few situations more appalling than fire at sea. By completely dieselizing *Varua* we have eliminated the greatest fire and explosion hazard—gasoline. Even the galley range, a No. 10140 Shipmate, is diesel. Thus there is only one fuel aboard ship, outside of a small tank of kerosene for emergency lighting in case of failure of electricity and for the Primus stove we carry aboard for this eventuality. The Chile voyage was the first time this had ever been used, and then for the unexpected purpose of cabin heating. Engine room and galley have a built-in C-O-Two system, besides a big portable C-O-Two extinguisher and a couple of Pyrenes.

In frequented waters collision is a very real hazard for small craft. A lone helmsman dreaming out his watch with his eyes on the compass and the stars ahead is apt to be negligent about keeping watch astern, even though there is a standing order, as there is aboard *Varua*, to get up and look all around the horizon every half-hour when the clock strikes. Even before the recent law went into effect prescribing at last a white stern light for sailing vessels, we carried one anyway; but as this is of necessity so low it may be obscured at times we have in addition a fixture on the mainmast head which throws a ghostly light on our white masts, and incidentally is a great aid in sail handling at night. I am not sure of the legality of this additional light but I would rather be illegal than run down.

In case of hitting something with the bow, *Varua* has a watertight steel collision bulkhead between galley and forecastle which should enable her to keep afloat until temporary repairs can be made.

Our foremast ladders, which can be seen on the sail plan, have so many advantages and uses that they might be put under a special heading of "wonderful and obvious improvements hitherto overlooked or avoided on account of tradition." Just one thing—the great reduction in windage due to the elimination of ratlines—would more than justify their use. Their most important advantage is the

APPENDICES FOR THE PRACTICAL SAILOR

great increase in safety. Every cruising yacht should have a means of getting aloft in a hurry. *Varua*'s rig requires one man to go aloft frequently on the foremast. Anyone who has had previous experience will realize what a good solid footing on the centerline of the ship can mean, compared with the dangerous snapping and jerking one is subjected to on ratlines, plus the ever-present possibility of the seizings having chafed through or worked loose. *Varua*'s ladders are of extra-heavy-duty copper pipe. They also serve as fairleads for halyards and brails, and are very convenient for passing the gaskets around the foresail when it is brailed in against the mast. They serve the same purpose for the fore topsail and the two main upper staysails.

Obviously mast ladders present a problem if there is a gaff, but even then they might be worked out if the hoist is not too great, as has been done on *Varua* to allow the topsail yard to travel up and down. Anyone who has once sailed with ladders instead of ratlines will never want to be without them.

In case of unforeseen emergency we carry a 10-man balsa life raft with deep platform bottom and netting, and a 13½-foot boat. The boat is a fine seaworthy model which we designed after the old ships' yawl boats and built especially for *Varua*. Before each voyage it is stocked with water in tins, concentrated food, mast, sail, rudder, and oars. It is carried upside down on the cabin house for protection from seas, but could be rolled over quickly if needed.

The safety features of the ship are backed up by all the precautions I can think of. Slocum and others who have disappeared without trace, in proved seaworthy craft, are assumed to have been run down while sleeping. Singlehanders are obliged to let their ships take care of themselves while they sleep. We too occasionally let *Varua* sail herself when conditions are right, but there is always someone on watch. Even down in the empty wastes of the Southern Ocean we carried our lights every night. In bad weather the two girls were not allowed on deck except in the steering well, which is reached from the charthouse without going on deck.

RADIO

The increased electrical installation and general complication that would go with transmitting and radio-telephone equipment would seem to serve no practical purpose for us considering how remote we generally are from shore stations. We do want a radio receiver powerful enough to get navigational time signals no matter where we are. For years we had a durable National Model NC 100 receiver which was on the old *Florence C. Robinson* before the war, and afterward on *Varua* up through the voyage to Chile. At Panama we finally turned it in, still functioning, for a new National Model 183D.

SWINGING TABLE

It is impossible to exaggerate the comfort and convenience of a properly designed swinging table. Suffice to say that during the entire thirteen years of *Varua's* existence there has never been a meal when the table has not been set normally, regardless of weather. The table has no rolling rails or battens. The only concession we have ever made, even in the worst weather, is to use a damp cloth on the table to prevent the possibility of things sliding.

WATER

This is no longer a problem. With modern tanks of noncorrosive metal, water will keep as long as you want. We had to accept galvanized tanks (galvanized after welding) due to priorities when building, but even with these we have had no trouble. We use Aquaclear regularly to protect the inside of the tanks. There is no way of knowing whether we might have had trouble without it. We have 625 gallons with tanks full. This is two months' supply for the ship, with practically no restrictions. I made a check recently on the voyage from Panama to Mangareva. We used 587 gallons in 52 days, about 11⅓ gallons per day, for five adults and a baby. Except for the girls' hair washing, we used all we wanted for all purposes, including even fresh-water showers, which require surprisingly little if care is used. When our supply is getting low we bathe by the sponge-and-dipper method, using less than a gallon. With salt-water soaps and detergents, sea water can be used more effectively than before, but is still far behind fresh water. If necessary, our water supply could be made to last four months without hardship.

CHAFE

People are always writing about the problem of chafe on a long voyage. We have practically eliminated chafe on *Varua* through the design of the rig and attention to the lead of all blocks, halyards, sheets, etc. Every line that does not lead straight from its block to the belaying pin is led through a lignum vitae fairlead. Of the fore and aft sails only the mainsail and No. 3 staysail can touch anything. The shrouds where these two sails touch are served with baggy wrinkle. The two squaresails have doublings stitched to the outer side where they rub the forestay and jibstay. The doublings can easily be replaced after a voyage.

The only damage from chafe that *Varua* has had for years was when the mainsail luff rope chafed through up near the head from a tight slide shackle. Since then the slide shackles do not pass around the luff rope any more, but go through rings seized to the sail. There is no chafe whatsoever now.

Every day at sea on the first morning watch after breakfast one of us makes a complete tour of the ship, and up the foremast, to check everything. There is no reason to go up the mainmast.

MAINTENANCE

Varua is run on a low budget. I keep one man aboard all the time. He gets $80 a month plus his food. For several years now it has been Tino, who is really a capable bosun's mate and can do everything from rigging, through sailmaking, to housekeeping. He actually lives aboard and is busy all the time. The only work we do not do ourselves is the semiannual hauling out for bottom painting, and twice in thirteen years an engine overhaul. When we go to sea we take one more along, basically as cook but to help on deck too. He gets the same pay.

There is hardly any varnish work. Most of the paint we mix ourselves, and as this makes a great difference in cost in the long run I mention our particular method. I do not like a hard gloss paint for the hull, for no matter what paint you use you have to repaint frequently on extended cruises. Hard paints build up a thick coat which eventually has to be burned or scraped off—an appalling job

TO THE GREAT SOUTHERN SEA

I never have to do, because I use a paint that chalks off as fast as I add new paint. My paint is made by mixing two parts of white lead or white zinc to one part linseed oil and one part turpentine. White lead is more opaque but chalks off fastest. White zinc is less opaque and more durable. If white lead chalks off too fast for you, use half and half lead and zinc.

For wire rigging I used to use warm linseed oil once a year. With *Varua*, which has white spars because they are cooler and because I like them that way, I now keep the rigging white too by rubbing it down with white lead and tallow, about one part to three parts, plus a little kerosene. Never use paint on wire rigging for it will crack and hold moisture inside.

INSECT CONTROL

It is absolutely unnecessary to have any bugs such as cockroaches aboard ship these days. All you need to do is to spray lockers and areas where bugs might live with a 5 per cent solution of D.D.T. or Chlordane in kerosene. This is a residual spray and will kill insects that touch it for several months from the time it is put on. You can also use D.D.T. dusting powder, blowing it behind sealings, into bilges, etc., with a hand duster.

MEDICAL EQUIPMENT

The cruising yachtsman cannot become a medical practitioner overnight, but he should have at least a medical kit, and some idea of what to do with it if needed. Here is a list of medical books in *Varua*'s library. The first book on the list, *The Ship's Medicine Chest and First Aid at Sea*, is probably the most valuable of all, for in addition to its medical and first-aid information it contains suggested lists for medical chests of various sizes all the way from lifeboat kits up to medical lockers for large ships.

> *The Ship's Medicine Chest and First Aid at Sea*—U. S. Public Health Service. Get latest edition.
> *Medical Care of Merchant Seamen*—W. L. Wheeler.
> *Red Cross Home Nursing*—The American Red Cross.

APPENDICES FOR THE PRACTICAL SAILOR

Red Cross First Aid Text Book—The American Red Cross.
Minor Surgery—Christopher.
Handbook of Physical Medicine—American Medical Association.
Health and Disease in the Tropics—Charles Wilcocks. (London)
Synopsis of Tropical Medicine—Manson-Bahr.

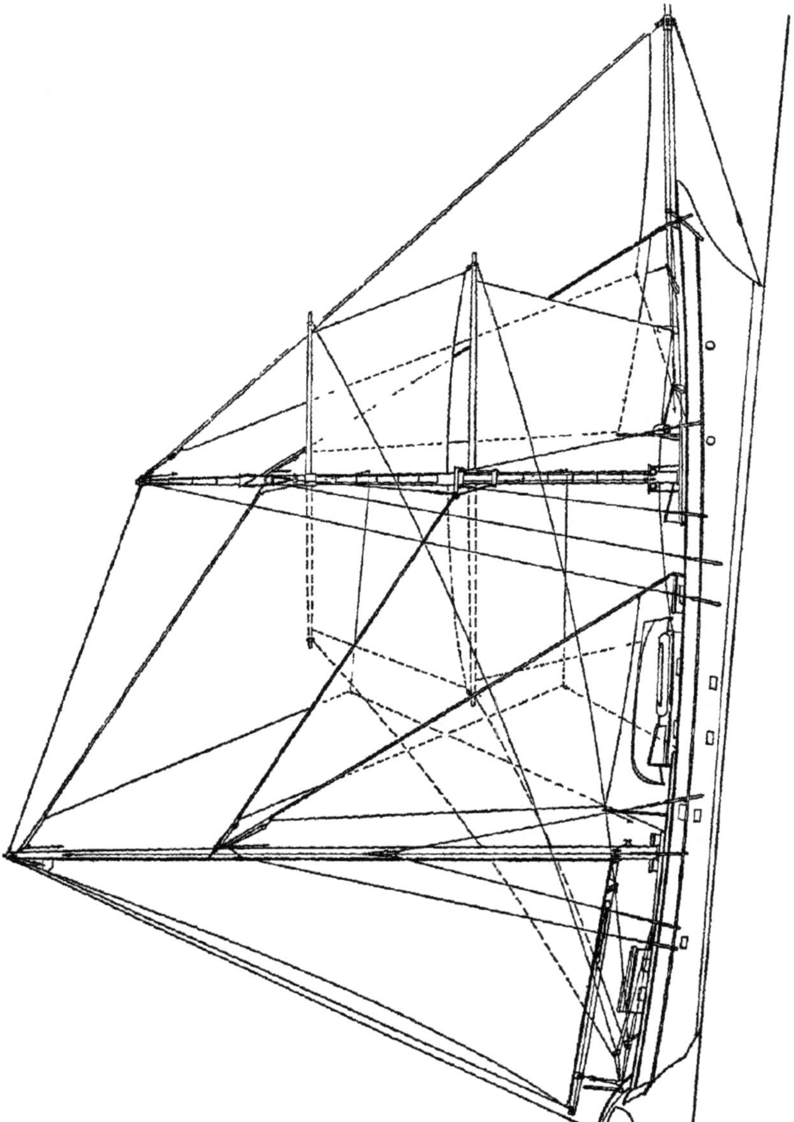

SAIL PLAN

Varua's sails are as follows (the system of numbers and weights of canvas being confusing, I have converted them all to ounces):

Fore staysail	205 sq. ft.,	12 oz.,	28½"	Commercial,	one bight
Lower main staysail	235 " "	"	"	"	" "
Jib	300 " "	10 "	"	"	" "
Mainsail	500 " "	"	"	"	" "
Foresail (Course)	470 " "	"	"	Wamsutta	" "
Middle main staysail	330 " "	8 "	"	Commercial	" "
Upper main staysail	320 " "	6 "	"	Boat Sail Drill	" "
Topsail	340 " "	3½ "	30"	Wamsutta	" "

The three staysails between the masts, listed above as lower main staysail, middle main staysail, and upper main staysail to avoid the complicated terms that might be applied by nautical purists, are usually referred to aboard *Varua* as No. 1, No. 2, and No. 3 staysails respectively.

There is also a storm mainsail, 300 sq. ft., and a storm fore staysail and main staysail of about 110 sq. ft. each. All are about 18 oz., made with one bight.

Our sails are on the light side, but all have extra tablings and reinforcements, and are usually roped all around. Jib, fore staysail, and main staysail have stainless steel luff wires.

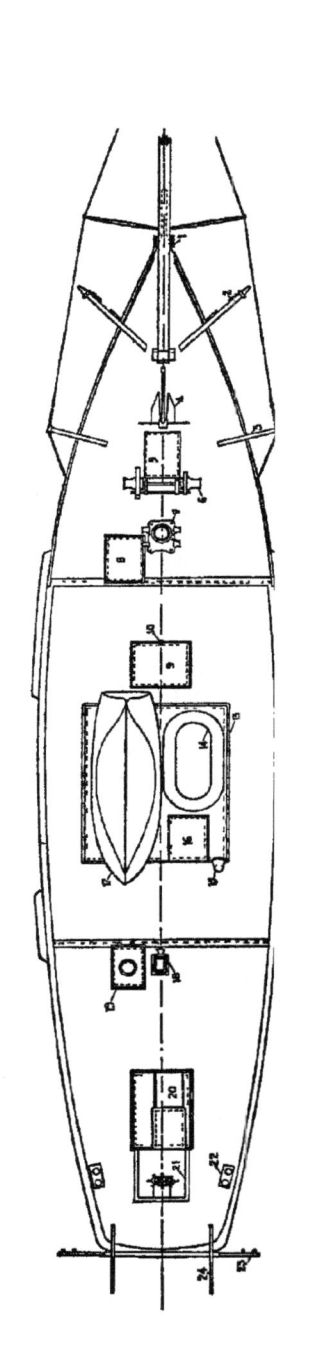

DECK PLAN

Varua's decks are remarkably clear. There are no fittings not shown on the plan.

1. Special fairlead wheels for anchor chains.
2. Forward catheads for working anchors, and to take jibsheets and square foresail tacks.
3. After catheads to take bowsprit shrouds, and jibsheet fairlead block.
4. 200-pound Danforth anchor. Another is stowed upright against mainmast, off the deck, and two more under the saloon divan.
5. Forecastle hatch.
6. Two-speed anchor windlass, hand operated.
7. Fife-rail around foremast, for belaying pins and halyard winches.
8. Galley hatch.
9. Engine-room hatch.
10. Chain plate for attachment of lower mainstay.
11. Channels for fore rigging.
12. Channels for main rigging.
13. Deckhouse over saloon.
14. 10-man balsa life raft.
15. Ventilator for bathroom.
16. Companionway to saloon.
17. 13½-foot boat.
18. Mainmast, with Merriman wire halyard winch.
19. Hatch over owner's stateroom.
20. Low house over navigation room.
21. Steering well.
22. After bitts.
23. Telescoping outriggers to take braces.
24. Combination stern davits and attachment for permanent backstays.

VENTILATION

Long ago I noticed that the natural tendency aboard ship is for reverse ventilation, that is, a flow from aft to forward. Instead of trying to fight this, as most yachts do in the arrangement of their hull openings, we planned *Varua* to foster it, and succeeded so well that there is an almost constant air stream through the ship. Twenty-five rectangular marine windows and four round air ports, strategically located in the deck breaks, houses, and in the hull itself, would by themselves give an exceptional amount of light and ventilation. But the real secret is in the sloping hatches, which cause the air to flow up and over them, creating a partial vacuum which draws the air out from below through the companionways. The chartroom hatch at the after end of the ship, being flat, does not have this effect, so the air enters at this point, flowing forward. Thus heat from the engine room and galley, and cooking smells, never come aft through the living quarters, even though all doors are open. Everything goes out through the galley hatch. The heat itself, rising through the galley hatch, causes a convection current and intensifies the flow of air through the ship.

In case one of the thwartship doors is closed, similar air circulation still goes on in each section of the ship for there are no dead ends, thanks to the breaks in the deck and the windows.

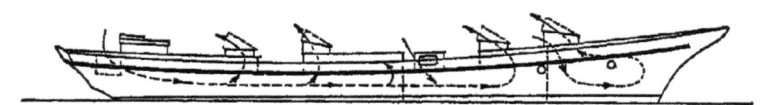

Almost invariably, under sail and at anchor, the flow of air follows the above pattern, which is simplified by showing only the main openings. Even with wind aft of the beam, the flow from the sails and the movement of the ship seem to divert the wind aft over the deck to set up the current described. About the only time this condition does not prevail is when moored stern to the wind, and when running directly before a strong wind. In this case, with the saloon door closed, the circulation in the galley and engine room will flow out of the engine hatch, and a separate circulation will be set up in the after part of the ship.

All this air might be less advantageous in a cold climate, although you can always close up if it is too drafty. It is, of course, the best possible insurance against dry rot.

ACCOMMODATION PLAN

Years of experience went into *Varua*'s accommodation plan. I wanted maximum comfort and privacy for one family and crew of two, with plenty of room for navigation, reference library and writing, auxiliary machinery, photographic laboratory, and stores. Strangers invariably ask, "How many does she sleep?" For years I had a kind of perverse pleasure in answering, "Two, and a crew of two." People would react as if it were slightly immoral to devote a 70-foot vessel to so few people.

Recently, what was a walk-in linen room and hanging closet opposite the bathroom, was converted to a children's cabin, and surprisingly managed to retain quite a lot of the shelf and hanging space.

Actually, the transom in the chartroom where I bed down sometimes in bad weather, and the berth in the storeroom off the galley, plus various other transoms and the divan, would allow another owner to "sleep" quite a few. For us she is a one-family boat and floating workshop.

For tropical living, distinct from voyaging, we required more than the usual light and air without endangering the ship in bad weather. This was accomplished by breaks in the deck, where we installed Rostand rectangular marine windows, with similar windows in house sides and ends, and—most unorthodox—windows in the hull itself. The latter have always aroused comment. They have proved safe and give a remarkably pleasant effect to the living quarters. A window falls just beside the head of each berth in the owner's stateroom, so one can look out while in bed. Carefully located and designed hatches and companionways provide remarkable through ventilation. There are no skylights, which I consider inefficient and leaky devices.

The working part of the ship, which is all forward, can be closed off by the saloon door, since there is separate access. Except for serving meals there is no need for through traffic.

Altogether it is a specialized, unconventional plan. To the average

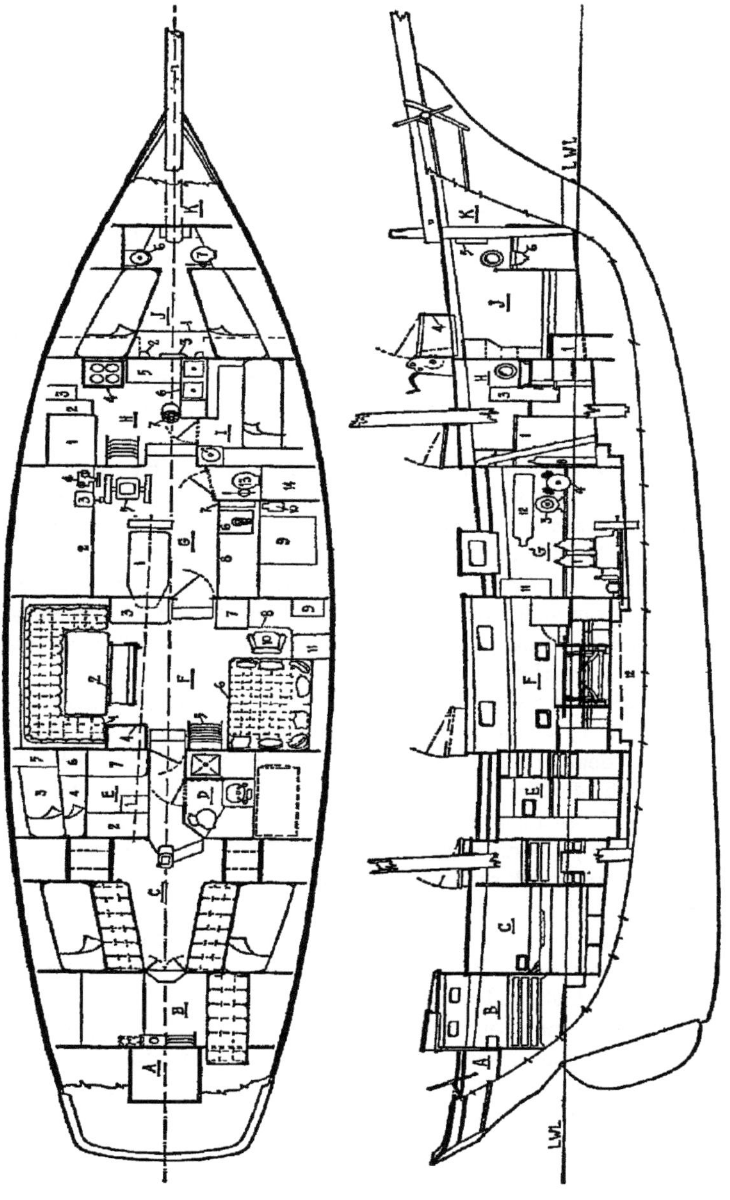

APPENDICES FOR THE PRACTICAL SAILOR

owner, accustomed to having guests aboard, it may seem a selfish plan. It is ideal for the purposes for which it was designed.

The following index explains the letters and numbers on the plan:

A *Self-draining steering well.* Small and deep to protect helmsman. Holds little water if a sea is shipped.

B *Navigation room.* Binnacle mounted inside on after bulkhead, slightly to port, seen through small window as was customary on Gloucester fishermen. Chronometers under glass in after end of large chart table to port. Large chart drawers under. Navigation books on forward bulkhead. In bad weather or complicated waters, navigator can nap within a few feet of helm on transom berth. Large open storage space around steering well reached easily from navigation room.

C *Owner's cabin.* Two steps down from navigation room. Two berths with large cushioned seats. Dressing tables each side of mainmast, with drawers over and under. Bookshelves on after bulkhead, both sides. 75-gallon water tanks under berths.

D *Bathroom.* Groco electric W.C.; Crane pullman lavatory with hot water from galley range; shower with seat like sitz bath. Medical stores on after bulkhead. 120-gallon water tank on outboard side with large linen shelves over.

E *Children's room.* Floor slightly raised to clear off-center propeller shaft. 1) Chest of drawers with buffet top, handy for baby's meals. 2) Seat or small child's berth, locker under. 3) Full-length upper berth. 4) Short lower berth for child. 5) Shelf over foot of berth. 6) Full-length hanging locker which can be shortened to allow full-length berth when required. 7) Dresser with drawers under, mirror and small shelves on forward bulkhead.

F *Main saloon.* Low deckhouse allows saloon floor to be raised, giving increased width of floor as well as fine headroom. A remarkably spacious room with marine windows on all four sides of house, as well as in hull itself at eye level when seated. This room, where much time is spent and where one eats, was deliberately placed where the motion is least. 1) Comfortable seat around table, with bookshelves back of all three sides. 2) Weighted swinging table. 3) Secretary-bureau. 4) Buffet. 5) Companion ladder. 6) Wide lounging divan. 7) Filing cabinet, hi-fi amplifier over. 8) Desk. Hinged section of top conceals automatic record player. Loud-speaker in bulkhead over desk. 9) National Model NC 183D radio receiver; typewriter stows under. 10) Chair. 11) Second filing cabinet. 12) Water tanks under floor, 350 gallons.

G *Engine room.* Photographic laboratory on starboard side. 1) Main engine, Deutz 47 h.p., two cycle, two cylinder, 600 r.p.m. 2) Large workbench over 310-gallon diesel fuel tank. 3) Dynamo. 4) Air compressor. 5) 5 h.p. Lister diesel to drive 3 and 4. 6) Photographic enlarger. 7) Switchboard. 8) Photographic laboratory over 450-gallon diesel fuel tank. 9) 32-volt batteries. 10) Converter. 11) 30-gallon diesel fuel day tank. 12) Air tank for starting main engine. 13) Hand pump W.C. 14) 40-gallon lube oil tank and engine spare parts.

H *Galley.* Large hatchway overhead gives excellent ventilation. There is also a porthole just beside the range. Large storage area under raised floor. 1) Icebox with shelves over. 2) Dresser and shelves. 3) 20-gallon hot-water tank with coil inside range. 4) Diesel oil Shipmate range No. 10140. Hood over range passes most of heat out through same stack with combustion gases. 5) Dresser with drawers and shelves under, and bins for dishes over. 6) Two deep sinks and drainboard. 7) Foremast. Excellent to lean against in a seaway. 8) C-O-Two bottles for fire-extinguishing system.

I *This is basically a storeroom.* Shelves from deck to deck for packaged and canned foods, and large bins for bulk stores. With a high berth over the bins, and a small corner lavatory, it now also provides occasional quarters for a child.

J *Forecastle and crew's washroom.* There are large shelves on the watertight steel bulkhead separating this room from the galley. 1) Chain locker for both port and starboard chains. 2) Chain lead pipes, both port and starboard. 3) Forecastle ladder. 4) Strong forecastle hatch, serving also as support for windlass. Side flaps allow this hatch to be open in almost any weather. 5) Crew's medicine cabinet. 6) Crew's lavatory. 7) Crew's W.C.

K *Fore peak.*

APPENDIX 2 — THE STORM

THE STORM

I have referred to our storm down south as the culminating experience of my life at sea, so it is only natural to return to it once more. I wish that we had had an anemometer aboard to check the wind velocity. Within the range that one is familiar with, say up to moderate gale force, one can estimate fairly closely. When you reach force ten Beaufort, which is whole gale, with winds of 55-63 miles per hour, and go beyond into the range which loosely contains storm and hurricane, I don't think anyone can claim to judge with anything approaching accuracy. One's perspective from a small vessel tends to produce exaggeration, which I have always tried to avoid through underestimating. All I can say is that this storm was way beyond the range of anything I had experienced before.

We were in a region where great seas were to be expected. Tannehill states: "In the South Pacific . . . near the 50th parallel, there is an unbroken sweep of the sea around the world, and here some very great waves are sometimes observed." Reference is made in this and other works to great waves up to ninety, even 112 feet in height. We saw no such monsters, if they really exist, but we saw some pretty big seas. During the height of the storm I was too occupied to measure wave heights. Afterward, when I had turned the wheel over to Tino, I measured them from the mast by the conventional method of sighting the horizon across the top of the nearest wave when we were at the bottom of the trough, and measuring my height of eye above the water. The seas had gone down considerably from the height they had reached during the night when the blow was at its worst. It was hard to get an accurate horizon, but a conservative average of my measurements showed that they were still running forty feet high. It is not unreasonable to estimate that they were in the vicinity of fifty feet high during the peak hours. The Hydrographic Office states that the relationship between height of seas and wind velocity is 1:2.05 which would put the wind at around a hundred miles an hour.

The thing that impressed me even more than the height of the waves was the short distance between them. For open waters such as these, the H. O. gives twenty times the height as the formula for length of seas, or 1,000 feet for fifty-foot waves. Even the forty-foot seas that I measured when the storm was on the wane would have been 800 feet apart according to this, whereas I don't think they were half that. This was the reason they were dangerous.

The fact that the storm, which was from northwest at its peak, was blowing against a heavy swell left over from the succession of easterly gales we had previously experienced, would in itself account for something rather spectacular in the way of seas.

Aside from contributing factors, such as conflicting swells and current, the length of seas in the open ocean depends upon the "fetch": the distance from the weather shore or from the center of the disturbance, whichever happens to be nearest. In our case the nearest land to windward was some 5,000 miles away, so the true fetch was the radius of the storm itself. From the steep barometric incline and other characteristics of the storm it was obviously a cyclonic disturbance of great intensity but short radius, and thus a deceptively short fetch.

It would have been interesting to know what this distance was. In the New England hurricane of September 1938, which I recorded in Gloucester harbor, there was a drop of a half-inch (from 30″ to 29.5″) in about eight hours, followed by a rise of a half-inch in twelve hours, after which it leveled off. In this case the center passed about seventy-five miles away.

In our storm there was almost identically the same drop, from the same level, in the same time. But afterward it took thirty-six hours to rise a half-inch and it kept on rising for another twenty-four hours. Possibly an expert could deduce how far we were from the center, and thus arrive at the fetch and a mathematical clue to the extreme shortness and steepness of the seas.

APPENDIX 3—RIDING OUT A STORM

RIDING OUT A STORM

For those who would like to know more about the reasoning behind my handling of *Varua* in the storm, I offer the following remarks. To begin with, I have no argument with the conventional methods of riding out the average gale encountered in summer cruising. This discussion is concerned with the handling of an able seagoing yacht faced with weather of such extreme proportions that the actual survival of the ship is involved. The usual advice, which is to keep the vessel's bow heading into the seas by the use of some form of sea anchor, raises the practical question whether or not this can be accomplished under extreme conditions.

With small, shoal-draft craft, including lifeboats, the major forces involved are wind pressure and the action of the surface water. Since both are moving in the same direction, it is reasonable to expect such a craft to tail out from its sea anchor and head into wind and sea. Strains are limited and the sea anchor can be kept to a reasonable size. Similar results would be obtained from any kind of drag, but in this case the sea anchor is convenient, and its intelligent use will offer the best chance of survival.

In larger, deeper hulls, another major force is present which changes the picture: solid water that is not moving to leeward. The greatest effort of wind and wave crests is exerted on the forward part of the ship, which has the least grip on solid water. Thus as the vessel makes sternway as it is bound to do while riding to a sea anchor, the bow falls off, pivoting on the after part of the hull which has a deeper grip on the water. It may be possible to arrest this with a riding sail and hold her in a position four or five points from the wind; but in extreme conditions, even if it were possible to have a riding sail and gear strong enough, the sail is becalmed when in the trough, and ineffective. A large breaking sea can throw you broadside to, at the mercy of the following crest. Do what you may, you will find the position untenable, for in the final analysis you are fighting against all the natural forces involved.

The unfortunate part about it all is that you have to commit yourself before it gets too bad, and once committed to the sea anchor over the bow you are stuck with it. You cannot at the peak of the storm decide to try the other system if yours is not working. You have abandoned all control over your ship. You are not in an enviable position.

Voss, the leading exponent of sea anchors, unwittingly gives innumerable arguments *against* them, as can be discovered by a careful analysis of the latter part of his book. Not the least of these is the fact that after all his experience with *Tilikum*—which never met the ultimate storm—he was unable to provide a sea anchor that would stand up when he finally did meet it years later in *Sea Queen,* a yacht of only nineteen feet waterline. I could cite innumerable examples of small yachts besides *Sea Queen* whose sea anchors broke up, or chafed loose, or spun themselves and their gear into a useless mess. If it is practically impossible to produce a sea anchor that will survive an extreme emergency for craft of only nineteen or twenty feet waterline, how is one expected to succeed in the larger sizes where the strains become enormous, and the gear of necessity cumbersome?

While speaking of Voss, he mentions several examples of large vessels, as well as little *Sea Queen,* that found themselves greatly relieved, and probably saved, when forced by loss of sea anchor or power to stop trying to hold themselves into the battering sea, and drifted with it instead. The same author also admits losing rudderposts twice from making sternway in vessels drifting to a sea anchor. Similar accidents too numerous to mention have occurred to others under similar conditions. No worse strain can be put on a rudder than to have the vessel surge and pitch against it when making sternway in a heavy sea.

In spite of these facts most yachtsmen still appear reluctant to consider running an acceptable maneuver in a gale, probably due to reiterated warnings against running too long, pooping, and broaching to. This whole subject is misunderstood generally, for the caution should be not against the act of running downwind, but against doing it too fast.

APPENDICES FOR THE PRACTICAL SAILOR

Conor O'Brien, who made a magnificent eastward voyage around the world in the 42-foot *Saoirse,* most of it running before the gales of high southern latitudes to round both Cape of Good Hope and Cape Horn, wrote that he "never met a sea before which Saoirse would not run safely." He would even run under sail until she began to make seas break astern, after which he would "check her way to insure against broaching to or pooping."

Another thing: the business of oil bags that one is supposed to haul out to the sea anchor with a neat little block and line. I defy anyone to lay down and maintain an oil slick from a sea anchor in tremendous breaking seas. Even if it were possible to prevent the gear from getting fouled up or chafed loose it would be suicide to work in the eyes of the ship.

In sum—in spite of tradition and wishful thinking—common sense and practical experience add up to the fact that meeting a really bad storm head on with a sea anchor is not only impractical, but dangerous.

Most experienced masters, in vessels of any size, generally ride out bad weather hove to under storm sails. They can carry canvas and gear heavy enough to stand it, and outside of exceptional circumstances will not be totally becalmed in the trough. But for small- and medium-sized vessels, and even large ones in really extreme conditions, what to do?

Once I had worked sea anchors out of my system, years ago, I discovered that the best thing to do when the seas got too high for riding sails was to let the vessel take a natural drift under bare poles. In the vessels I have owned this was slightly downwind with the seas on the quarter. This was successful and safe under the worst conditions I had seen on previous voyages. Even so, I felt that it was not the whole story.

All my experience and thinking told me that if we ever met a really climactic storm some day it would have to be met end on—specifically end on, not a few points one way or another. Before the storm down south, this was purely theory. Since then I know I was right. Those seas were not normal seas. Unusual conditions caused them to be disproportionately high for their length, almost perpendicular, with great overhanging crests that broke many feet deep. But abnormal or not, they were there, and we had to meet them. It would have been folly, even in a large ship, to have met

Perhaps the thing is to coin a phrase "drift tendency": the tendency of the vessel to drift with the bow upwind, downwind, or broadside to in a heavy wind with the rudder amidships and no drags. Any yacht can try it out at sea. Knowing this, it would seem logical to follow whichever procedure will help her natural drift tendency, rather than fight it, for in the final extremity the natural forces will take over in spite of all you do, and it is better at that point to be working with, not against, them, to retain some degree of control over your fate. Thus, if she has an upwind drift tendency, which is most unlikely, it might be better to meet seas bow on, and take a chance on the extra strains on the rudder. If she has a negative or downwind drift tendency, I would keep her headed downwind with drags as described.

If your ship is already built, and is designed to take a breaking sea with either end, you have no problem. If it would be dangerous to meet breaking seas with your particular type of stern you will have to meet them with the bow as best you can.

These suggestions are not offered as hard and fast rules, but rather as my own views after an encounter with the greatest storm of twenty-five years of voyaging. There is little likelihood that one yacht in ten, following the usual routes, will ever encounter what I have been calling the ultimate storm, but just on the chance that she might, and that I could be right, it would perhaps be worthwhile to give careful thought to the design and arrangement of the stern of your dream ship.